D1559735

Hong Kong

Restaurants & Hotels

LOCAL EDITORS
Rory Boland and Angie Wong

STAFF EDITOR
Yoji Yamaguchi

Published and distributed by
Zagat Survey, LLC
4 Columbus Circle
New York, NY 10019
T: 212.977.6000
E: china@zagat.com
www.zagat.com

ACKNOWLEDGMENTS

We thank An Ping Cao, Dick Catlin, Edwin Chan, Rahul Dansanghani, Tom Davies, Cameron Dueck, David Gallie, Caroline Hatchett, Carolyn Heller, Alice and Roger King, Diana and Stephen King, Mary Pei, Roberta Pei, Steven Shukow, Henry and Patricia P. Tang, Michael Tong and Amy Vlastelica, as well as the following members of our staff: Chris Miragliotta (editorial project manager), Amy Cao (editorial assistant), Brian Albert, Sean Beachell, Maryanne Bertollo, Sandy Cheng, Reni Chin, Larry Cohn, Bill Corsello, Carol Diuguid, Curt Gathje, Alison Flick, Jeff Freier, Karen Hudes, Roy Jacob, Natalie Lebert, Mike Liao, Dave Makulec, Andre Pilette, Josh Rogers, Kimberly Rosado, Becky Ruthenburg, Donna Marino Wilkins, Sharon Yates, Anna Zappia and Kyle Zolner.

The reviews published in this guide are based on public opinion surveys. The numerical ratings reflect the average scores given by all survey participants who voted on each establishment. The text is based on direct quotes from, or fair paraphrasings of, participants' comments. Phone numbers, addresses and other factual information were correct to the best of our knowledge when published in this guide.

Contents

Ratings & Symbols

Ratings and Reviews

All **ratings** throughout this guide are on the Zagat 0 to 30 scale as follows:

0	–	9	poor to fair
10	–	15	fair to good
16	–	19	good to very good
20	–	25	very good to excellent
26	–	30	extraordinary to perfection
	∇		low response | less reliable

Ratings apply to the key aspects of each category covered: Food, Decor and Service in the Dining category; Rooms, Service, Dining and Facilities for Hotels.

Cost is covered differently, as noted in the Ratings & Symbols keys at the beginning of each section.

Surveyor comments are shown in quotation marks within reviews.

Symbols

Z	Zagat Top Spot (highest ratings, popularity and importance)
◗	serves after 11 PM
S	closed on Sunday
M	closed on Monday
⊄	no credit cards accepted

See also the Ratings & Symbols key in the Hotels section.

About This Survey

Here are the results of our **Hong Kong Restaurants & Hotels Survey,** covering 173 restaurants and 36 hotels as rated by 1,328 local surveyors. Like all of our guides, this one is based on the collective opinions of savvy consumers.

WHO PARTICIPATED: Of these surveyors, 41% are women, 59% men; the breakdown by age is 11% in their 20s; 33%, 30s; 23%, 40s; 18%, 50s; 15%, 60s (their comments are shown in quotation marks within the reviews). We sincerely thank each of these participants – this book is really "theirs."

OUR EDITORS: Special thanks go to our local editors: Rory Boland, a Warsaw- and Hong Kong–based freelance writer, and Angie Wong, food editor at *Time Out Hong Kong.*

ABOUT ZAGAT: This marks our 29th year reporting on the shared experiences of consumers like you. Today we have well over 300,000 surveyors and now cover dining, lodging, shopping and tourist attractions worldwide.

SHARE YOUR OPINION: Join any of our upcoming surveys – just register at **ZAGAT.com,** where you can rate and review establishments year-round, and get a free copy of the resulting guide when published.

AVAILABILITY: Zagat guides are available in all major bookstores, by subscription at **ZAGAT.com** and for use on web-enabled mobile devices via **ZAGAT TO GO** or **ZAGAT.mobi.**

FEEDBACK: There is always room for improvement, thus we invite your comments and suggestions about any aspect of our performance. Is there something more you would like us to include in our guides? Did we get anything wrong? Just contact us at **china@zagat.com.**

New York, NY
May 2008

Nina and Tim

Nina and Tim Zagat

A Visitor's Primer

A former British colony and now a Special Administrative Region of China, a city with its own currency and laws, Hong Kong is a fascinating study in contrasts – East and West, old and new, colonial and cosmopolitan, exotic and high-tech. One of the world's major financial capitals, Hong Kong is also a hotbed of art, culture and fashion. It's no surprise that millions of visitors flock here annually.

GETTING AROUND: Hong Kong is located in the **Pearl River Delta.** In addition to some 260 outlying islands, it consists of four main areas: **Hong Kong Island, Kowloon Peninsula, Lantau Island** and the **New Territories.** Victoria Harbour separates Kowloon from Hong Kong Island; bordering it on Hong Kong Island are Central, the main business district, and Wan Chai and Causeway Bay, vibrant cultural centers; and on Kowloon, Tsim Sha Tsui. The New Territories are popular for their beaches, hiking trails and parks. Public transportation is fast and cheap. The Mass Transit Railway (MTR), which connects Hong Kong Island to Kowloon, is considered the best way to travel through the peninsula, while the equally efficient Kowloon Canton Railway (KCR) connects to the New Territories. Hong Kong Island is also served by a distinctive fleet of double-decker trams. Taxi fares start at around HKD15 for the first 2km, HKD1.40 for each additional 200 meters.

WHEN TO VISIT: Hong Kong's subtropical climate is most comfortable in fall, when days are warm and humidity is relatively low. Winters are for the most part mild, spring brings fog and rain, and summers are relentlessly sweltering, with occasional typhoon activity. Of course, the off-season usually translates into lower hotel rates.

HOLIDAYS: The major Chinese holidays are New Year, aka Spring Festival (the next dates are January 26, 2009, and February 14, 2010), and two Golden Weeks, seven-day holidays that fall around Labor Day (May 1) and National Day (October 1). In addition, one of the crown jewels of the rugby world, the Hong Kong Sevens tournament, takes place on the last weekend of March. During these periods, hotels are flooded with visitors.

ATTRACTIONS: Hong Kong's most famous attraction is the **Peak** in Central, the highest point on Hong Kong Island, which boasts shopping and dining along with picture-postcard views. Remarkable views can also be had from any window overlooking **Victoria Harbour,** which separates Kowloon from Hong Kong Island. One of the deepest natural ports in the world and the hub of much of Hong Kong's commercial and cultural activity, it teems with an incredible range of boats, from Chinese junks to container ships and everything in-between. No trip to Hong Kong would be complete without a ride across the harbor on the **Star Ferry.** Other popular attractions include Tsim Sha Tsui's waterfront **Promenade,** where you can watch nightly laser shows as well as seasonal fireworks, and to sate your cultural cravings, the **Museum of Art** and **Museum of History,** also in Tsim Sha Tsui. While few may associate Hong Kong with nature preserves, **Kowloon Park** in Tsim Sha Tsui and the **Hong Kong Wetlands Park** in the New Territories offer natural refuges from the urban landscape. And for more contemplative experiences, there are **Man Mo,** Hong Kong's oldest Taoist temple, in Sheung Wan; the **10,000 Buddhas Monastery** in Shatin; and the massive **Tian Tan Buddha** on Lantau Island. Families with kids can check out **Hong Kong Disneyland,** also on Lantau, or **Ocean Park** in Aberdeen. If you're interested in gambling, Macau is only one hour away by hydrofoil.

DINING: Hong Kong has long been an Asian food haven. Now more than ever, it's embracing its national roots. While Hong Kongers are excited about modern Chinese cuisine that mixes traditional cooking with global ingredients, as practiced at **Lung King Heen,** voted No. 1 for Food by our surveyors, traditionalists such as **Fook Lam Moon** also remain big draws. And high quality doesn't always translate into high prices, with places such as the Shanghainese **Crystal Jade** (Hong Kong's Best Buy) and the Cantonese **Dim Sum The Art of Chinese Tidbits** serving

Dining Glossary

Many restaurants in China have English menus – but that doesn't necessarily make ordering easy, given sometimes poor translations and the intricacies of authentic Chinese cuisines. Here is a brief glossary in pinyin.

REGIONAL CUISINES AND THEIR SIGNATURE DISHES

Cantonese (Yue), including Hong Kong
- **cha shao:** barbecue pork (dim sum)
- **cha shao bao:** barbecue pork buns (dim sum)
- **dan ta:** egg tarts (dim sum)
- **dim sum:** small snacks, usually served in bamboo steamers
- **niuliu chao hefen:** beef stir-fried with rice noodles
- **pidan shourou zhou:** rice porridge with preserved egg and pork
- **shao e:** roast goose
- **shao mai:** pork and shrimp dumplings (dim sum)
- **xia jiao:** shrimp dumplings (dim sum)
- **yu ci:** shark's fin
- **zibao ji:** paper-wrapped chicken

Hakka (Kejia), from a Chinese minority known for its use of lighter flavors
- **bingsha:** shaved-ice (dessert)
- **san bei ji:** three-cup chicken with sesame oil, soy sauce and rice wine
- **taisi lurou:** braised fatty pork

Hunanese (Xiang), the spiciest
- **duojiao yutou:** chopped chile fish head
- **la rou:** aged sausage

Northern (Beifang), including Beijing
- **basi pingguo:** candied apples
- **Beijing kaoya:** Peking duck
- **guo tie:** potstickers
- **jiaozi:** dumplings
- **jing jiang rousi:** shredded pork in soybean wrappers
- **lü da guan'r:** sweet rice gluten with red bean paste (dessert)
- **shuan yangrou:** lamb hot pot
- **tang cu liji:** vinegar and sugar pork
- **tudou si:** shredded potatoes with garlic (appetizer)
- **xiang la zha tudou si:** spicy fried shoestring potatoes

Sichuan (Chuan)
- **chaoshou:** spicy won tons

dan dan mian: noodles with chile oil, ground pork and preserved vegetables

gongbao jiding: spicy chicken stir-fried with peanuts

huiguo rou: twice-cooked pork belly

kou shui ji: spicy cold chicken (appetizer)

lazi ji: deep-fried chicken with red chiles

mapo doufu: spicy tofu with ground beef

mayi shang shu: glass noodles with ground meat and chiles

shui zhu niurou: beef cooked in hot oil

shui zhu yu: fish cooked in hot oil

Xinjiang, from the Muslim province, known for its use of cumin and lamb

la tiao zi: spicy noodles

nang: oven-baked bread

yangrou chuan: lamb skewers

Yangtze River Delta (Huaiyang), including Shanghai

babao fan: eight-treasure rice

dazha xie: small hairy crabs, steamed and served with vinegar

dongpo rou: red-braised pork with yellow cooking wine

hongshao: red-braising method utilizing soy sauce and sugar

hongshao qiezi: red-braised eggplant

kao fu: spongy wheat gluten with soy sauce (appetizer)

shizi tou: meatball made with pork and crab meat

shuijin xia: crystal shrimp, lightly stir-fried

zui ji: drunken chicken (appetizer)

Yunnan, unique for its Thai-influenced flavors

guoqiao mixian: cross-bridge noodles

qi guo ji: steamed chicken in a clay pot

TERMS

beef: **niu rou**

beer: **pi jiu**

bitter: **ku**

chicken: **ji rou**

Chinese cuisine: **Zhong can**

chopsticks: **kuai zi**

coffee: **ka fei**

dessert: **tian dian**

fish: **yu**

fork: **cha zi**

ginger: **jiang**

knife: **dao**

menu: **cai dan**

MSG: **weijing**

napkin: **canjing zi**

noodles: **mian**

pepper, usually white ground: **hujiao**

pork: **zhu rou**

rice: **mi fan**

salt: **yan**

salty: **xian**

smoking area: **xi yan qu**

    nonsmoking area: **fei xi yan qu**

soup: **tang**

sour: **suan**

soy sauce: **jiang you**

spicy: **la**

spoon: **shao**

sugar: **tang**

sweet: **tian**

tea: **cha**

    green tea: **lü cha**

    jasmine tea: **moli hua cha**

    oolong tea: **wu long cha**

    pearl milk tea: **zhenzhu naicha**

vegetables: **shu cai**

vegetarian food: **su shi**

waiter/waitress: **fuwu yuan**

water: **shui**

    boiled hot water: **re kai shui**

    bottled water: **kuan quan shui**

    cold water: **bing shui**

Western (non-Chinese) cuisine: **xi can**

wine: **putao jiu**

    red wine: **hong putao jiu**

    white wine: **bai putao jiu**

wok: **guo**

HELPFUL PHRASES

Bu chi la: I don't eat spicy foods.

Buyao fang weijing: Don't add MSG.

Maidan: Check, please.

Wo zhi chi su shi: I'm a vegetarian.

DINING

MOST POPULAR

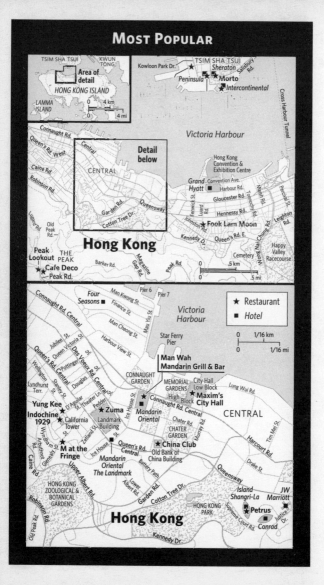

subscribe to ZAGAT.com

Most Popular Restaurants

1. Felix | *Continental*
2. Yung Kee | *Chinese*
3. Gaddi's | *French*
4. Nobu | *Japanese*
5. Spoon | *French*
6. Lobby at Peninsula | *Eclectic/English*
7. Mandarin Grill | *Eclectic*
8. Peak Lookout | *Continental/Eclectic*
9. China Club | *Chinese*
10. M at the Fringe | *French/Med.*
11. Aqua | *Italian/Japanese*
12. Morton's | *Steak*
13. Hutong | *Chinese*
14. Petrus | *French*
15. Fook Lam Moon | *Chinese*
16. Maxim's City Hall | *Chinese*
17. Cafe Deco | *Asian/Continental*
18. Zuma | *Japanese*
19. Man Wah | *Chinese*
20. Indochine 1929 | *Vietnamese*

Top Food Ratings

Excludes places with low votes, unless indicated by a ▽.

28	Lung King Heen	*Chinese* Sushi Hiro	*Japanese*
27	Gaddi's	*French* Petrus	*French* L'Atelier de Joël Robuchon	*French*
26	Fook Lam Moon	*Chinese* Morton's	*Steak* Nadaman	*Japanese* Da Domenico	*Italian* Yan Toh Heen	*Chinese*

Man Wah | *Chinese*
Spring Moon* | *Chinese*

25 Mandarin Grill | *Eclectic*
Caprice | *French*
1 Harbour Road | *Chinese*
Nobu | *Japanese*
Steak House | *Steak*
Gaia Ristorante | *Italian*
Dim Sum | *Chinese*
Inagiku | *Japanese*

BY CUISINE

CHINESE

28 Lung King Heen
26 Fook Lam Moon

Yan Toh Heen
Man Wah
Spring Moon*

* Indicates a tie with restaurant above

25 1 Harbour Road	**JAPANESE**
Dim Sum	28 Sushi Hiro
24 Lei Garden	26 Nadaman
Hutong	25 Nobu
Da Ping Huo	Inagiku
	24 Zuma

CONTINENTAL

- 22 Zest
- Amber
- 21 Felix
- Verandah, The
- 20 Press Room

MEDITERRANEAN/ MIDEASTERN

- 24 M at the Fringe
- 23 Scirocco∇
- 19 Beirut
- 16 Cococabana

ECLECTIC

- 25 Mandarin Grill
- 23 Café TOO
- 22 Lobby at Peninsula
- 20 Bo Innovation
- 19 Pearl on the Peak

SEAFOOD

- 23 Victoria City
- 20 Fish Bar
- Super Star
- 19 Dot Cod
- 16 Frog Faced Fish
- Jumbo Floating Rest.*

ENGLISH

- 23 Chinnery, The
- 22 Lobby at Peninsula
- Clipper Lounge
- 19 Dot Cod

STEAKHOUSES

- 26 Morton's
- 25 Steak House
- 22 Craftsteak
- 21 Ruth's Chris
- 18 Stonegrill∇

FRENCH

- 27 Gaddi's
- Petrus
- L'Atelier de Joël Robuchon
- 25 Caprice
- 24 M at the Fringe

THAI/VIETNAMESE

- 22 Nha Trang
- Indochine 1929
- 20 Lian
- Thai Basil
- 18 Rice Paper

ITALIAN

- 26 Da Domenico
- 25 Gaia Ristorante
- 23 Ciprani's
- Grissini
- Di Vino

subscribe to ZAGAT.com

BY SPECIAL FEATURE

BUFFET

24 Bombay Dreams
23 Café TOO
   Tiffin Lounge
22 Clipper Lounge
19 Spice Market

BUSINESS DINING

28 Lung King Heen
27 Gaddi's
   Petrus
   L'Atelier de Joël Robuchon
26 Nadaman

DINING ALONE

23 Chinnery, The
   Crystal Jade
22 Nha Trang
20 Lian
19 Habibi

FAMILY-STYLE PORTIONS

28 Lung King Heen
25 1 Harbour Road
24 Lei Garden
   Hutong
23 Yung Kee

HOTEL DINING

28 Lung King Heen
   (Four Seasons)
27 Gaddi's
   (Peninsula)
   Petrus
   (Island Shangri-La)
26 Morton's
   (Sheraton)
   Nadaman
   (Island Shangri-La)

LUNCH

28 Lung King Heen
   Sushi Hiro
27 Gaddi's
   Petrus
   L'Atelier de Joël Robuchon

MEET FOR A DRINK

24 Zuma
23 Chinnery, The
   Di Vino
22 Opia
   Isola

PEOPLE-WATCHING

25 Gaia Ristorante
22 Wagyu
19 Cinecittà
18 Dragon-I
17 Al's Diner

POWER SCENES

28 Lung King Heen
27 L'Atelier de Joël Robuchon
26 Nadaman
25 Mandarin Grill
22 Amber

QUIET CONVERSATION

27 Gaddi's
   Petrus
25 Caprice
24 M at the Fringe
22 Clipper Lounge

SINGLES SCENES

24 Zuma
23 Di Vino
22 Opia
   Isola
21 Felix

TRANSPORTING EXPERIENCES

24 Da Ping Huo
22 Maxim's City Hall
21 Felix
20 Bo Innovation
16 Jumbo Floating Rest.

VISITORS ON EXPENSE ACCOUNT

27 Gaddi's
   L'Atelier de Joël Robuchon

26 Morton's
   Da Domenico
25 Nobu

WINNING WINE LISTS

28 Lung King Heen
27 Gaddi's
   Petrus
   L'Atelier de Joël Robuchon
25 Mandarin Grill

BY LOCATION

ADMIRALTY

27 Petrus
26 Nadaman
23 Yè Shanghai
   Café TOO
   Nicholini's

CAUSEWAY BAY

28 Sushi Hiro
26 Da Domenico
23 Farm House
22 Opia
   Little Sheep

CENTRAL

28 Lung King Heen
27 L'Atelier de Joël Robuchon
26 Man Wah
25 Mandarin Grill
   Caprice

LAN KWAI FONG

22 Indochine 1929
20 Kee Club

19 Azure
   Beirut
17 Al's Diner

SOHO

24 Da Ping Huo
22 Craftsteak
20 Chez Patrick
   Boca Tapas & Wine
19 Yellow Door

TSIM SHA TSUI

27 Gaddi's
26 Morton's
   Yan Toh Heen
   Spring Moon
25 Nobu

WAN CHAI

26 Fook Lam Moon
25 1 Harbour Road
24 Lei Garden
23 Grissini
   Victoria City

Top Decor Ratings

28	Hutong		Petrus
27	Felix	25	Lumiere
	China Club		Spoon
	L'Atelier de Joël Robuchon		Verandah, The
	Caprice		Amber
	Lobby at Peninsula		Spring Moon
26	Gaddi's	24	Man Wah
	Yan Toh Heen		1 Harbour Road
	Zuma		Azure
	Aqua		Inagiku

OUTDOORS

Boathouse, The	Grill at Plateau
Cococabana	Isola
Dirty Duck	Peak Lookout
Fish Bar	RED
Gaia Ristorante	Stoep, The

ROMANCE

Amigo	Gough 40 Cafe
Aqua	M at the Fringe
Caprice	One-Thirtyone
Cococabana	Petit Pomerol
Gaia Ristorante	Verandah, The

TRENDY

Agnès B.	FINDS
Aqua	Green T. House
Azure	Ingredients
Dragon-I	Opia
Felix	Zuma

VIEWS

Aqua	Grill at Plateau
Boathouse, The	Isola
Cafe Deco	Peak Lookout
Caprice	Spoon
Felix	Tott's Grill & Bar

Top Service Ratings

29	Gaddi's		Lobby at Peninsula
			1 Harbour Road
28	Yan Toh Heen	25	Morton's
27	Petrus		Nadaman
	Spring Moon		Spoon
	Mandarin Grill		Clipper Lounge
26	Chinnery, The	24	Lung King Heen
	Caprice		Amigo
	Man Wah		Nicholini's
	L'Atelier de Joël Robuchon		M at the Fringe
	Steak House		

Best Buys

In order of Bang for the Buck rating.

1. Crystal Jade
2. Shake 'Em Buns
3. Maxim's City Hall
4. Nha Trang
5. Indonesian Rest. 1968
6. Chilli N Spice
7. Dim Sum
8. Al's Diner
9. Thai Basil
10. Lobby at Peninsula
11. Luk Yu Tea House
12. Boathouse, The
13. Rice Paper
14. Clipper Lounge
15. Little Sheep
16. McSorley's
17. China Tee Club
18. Di Vino
19. Spice Market
20. Boca Tapas & Wine

OTHER GOOD VALUES

Bizou Bistro
Chiu Chow Garden
Craftsteak
Mi-Ne Sushi
Modern China

Peak Bar
Scirocco
Song Cuisine d'Indochine
Tuk Tuk Thai
Wang Fu

Dining

Ratings & Symbols

Food, Decor and **Service** are rated on the Zagat 0 to 30 scale.

Cost reflects our surveyors' estimate of the price of dinner with one drink and tip and is a benchmark only. Lunch is sometimes 25% less. For places without ratings, cost in Hong Kong dollars is shown as follows:

I $149 and below
M $150 to $299
E $300 to $499
VE $500 or more

◐ serves after 11 PM
Ⓜ closed on Monday
Ⓢ closed on Sunday
⊄ no credit cards accepted

Agave Tequila Y Comida ◐ *Mexican* 10 | 14 | 15 | $199

Lan Kwai Fong | 33 D'Aguilar St. (Lan Kwai Fong) | (852) 2521-2010

"Killer margaritas" and what could be "Hong Kong's best and biggest tequila selection" draw "lively" types to this "well-located" Lan Kwai Fong Mexican with a prime "view of the strip"; the "reasonable", just-"ok" grub (including some 100 kinds of chili) is deemed about as authentic as the faux Santa Fe decor, but, hey – it "helps absorb the liquids."

NEW **Agnès B. Le Pain Grillé** *French* 15 | 18 | 13 | $311

Causeway Bay | Lee Gardens | 111 Leighton Rd. (Yun Ping Rd.) | (852) 2577-2718 | www.agnesb-lepaingrille.com

French clothier Agnès B. tries her hand at food with this "like-in-Paris" Causeway Bay Gallic bistro next to her boutique, a "pleasant" option for casual classics enjoyed amid furnishings mostly imported from France; though a few suspect something was "lost in the translation", citing "so-so" food and service, "when you need to eat and shop" it fills the bill.

Al's Diner ◐ *American* 17 | 14 | 13 | $173

Lan Kwai Fong | 27-39 D'Aguilar St. (Lan Kwai Fong) | (852) 2521-8714

Crowds of revelers "come for the Jell-O shots" and cheap beers at this "loud, happy" "neighborhood staple" in Lan Kwai Fong modeled after a

"1950s American diner" (complete with "kitschy" vinyl booths and neon); "homesick expats" say it's just the thing "when you crave a burger", "killer shake" or other "basic" comfort fare.

Amaroni's Little Italy *Italian*   15 | 16 | 17 | $241

Kowloon Tong | Festival Walk | 80 Tat Chee Rd. (Cornwall St.) | (852) 2265-8818 | www.danryans.com/amar

"Not Little Italy, but close", this roomy, "reliable" Kowloon Tong standby "satisfies cravings for chicken parm" and other "classic Americanized Italian" favorites dished up in "large portions" served "family-style"; factor in reasonable prices and "friendly" staffers willing to give "good advice on ordering", and no wonder it's so "difficult to book a table."

Amber *Continental/French*   22 | 25 | 23 | $748

Central | Mandarin Oriental The Landmark | 15 Queen's Rd. Central (Ice House St.) | (852) 2132-0066 | www.mandarinoriental.com

This tony Central hotel dining room's "spectacular" Adam Tihany-designed space featuring a dramatic hanging sculpture made of thousands of metal rods sets the stage for chef Richard Ekkebus' "innovative" "nouveau" French-Continental cuisine and *vins* chosen from an "interactive electronic list"; "attentive" pro service and the "best afternoon tea" are other pluses, and while it's all seriously "pricey", at least you're likely to "impress your client or date."

Amigo *French*   22 | 19 | 24 | $663

Happy Valley | 79A Wong Nai Chung Rd. (Blue Pool Rd.) | (852) 2577-2202 | www.amigo.com.hk

"Everyone celebrates birthdays and anniversaries" at this "romantic" institution across from the Race Course that's an "all-time favorite for old Hong Kongers", offering "reliable" "high-end" fare that's classic French – its moniker and digs in an 18th-century "Spanish colonial"-style house notwithstanding; a few upstarts call the "candlelit" quarters "dated" and the "impeccable" formal service "stuffy", but most maintain there's a reason it's been around "for decades."

Aqua *Italian/Japanese*   19 | 26 | 20 | $587

Tsim Sha Tsui | One Peking Rd. | 1 Peking Rd., 29th fl. (Kowloon Park Dr.) | (852) 3427-2288 | www.aqua.com.hk

The "stunning views of Hong Kong's skyline" never fail to "impress" at this 29th-floor Tsim Sha Tsui standout, while the service and cuisine featuring both Italian and Japanese dishes are also considered "good"; just don't be surprised if the tab "looks like a hedge fund buyout offer"; N.B. travel over Victoria Harbour in the Aqualuna, their wooden junk ship done up in 1930s-Shanghai style, for pre- or post-dinner drinks.

Avenue Restaurant & Bar *Continental*   - | - | - | E

Tsim Sha Tsui | Holiday Inn Golden Mile | 50 Nathan Rd. (Mody Rd.) | (852) 2523-2203 | www.holidayinn.com

Make plans to meet at this modern Continental in the Holiday Inn Golden Mile where abstract art graces the spacious interior, and floor-to-ceiling windows offer *the* view of Tsim Sha Tsui's bustling main thoroughfare; an elegant buffet of appetizers and desserts tempts lunchers awaiting their made-to-order entrees, but in the evening, à la carte is what's à la mode.

Azure *Continental*   19 | 24 | 15 | $508

Lan Kwai Fong | Hotel LKF | 33 Wyndham St., 29th fl. (D'Aguilar St.) | (852) 3518-9330 | www.azure.hk

"Fabulously located" on top of the Hotel LKF with "one of the best views over the harbor you can get", this posh, high-design Lan Kwai Fong supper club is an "alluring" choice for first dates or out-of-town guests; the modern Continental fare is deemed just "ok" and the service "uneven", but an impressive terrace and bar/lounge compensate.

Babek *Indian*   - | - | - | M

Soho | 9 Elgin St. (Hollywood Rd.) | (852) 2975-9332 | www.babek.hk

Though its name is spelled backwards, this creative Soho Indian does some forward thinking with an enticing four-course tasting menu starring those namesake skewered meats served straight from the sizzling tandoor oven to your plate; while every seat under the soaring ceiling buzzes over the test-tube lassis and modern fare, book a spot at the chic cinnamon-and-cream colored kebab bar for the full experience.

Baci Pizza *Italian*   17 | 12 | 14 | $247

Lan Kwai Fong | 1 Lan Kwai Fong, 2nd fl. (D'Aguilar St.) | (852) 2801-5885

Spread over three levels, this "friendly" Italian is in a location "tucked away from the Lan Kwai Fong crowds" yet boasts a compelling "view over all the action"; most "come here for the pizza" – its "thin-crust" pies are "perhaps the best in Central" – but there are also "simple pastas" and such.

	FOOD	DECOR	SERVICE	COST

Balalaika ● *Russian*

16 | 18 | 19 | $296

Lan Kwai Fong | LKF Tower | 33 Wyndham St. (D'Aguilar St.) | (852) 3579-2929 | www.kingparrot.com

You "can't help but feel Russki" as you don "fur coats and hats" and "down vodka shots" in the "minus 20-degrees Celcius" "ice room" that's the claim to fame of this Lan Kwai Fong Russian "theme" joint; ubiquitous taxidermied animal heads set the stage for its "tableside spears of meat" and other carnivore-friendly classic dishes, which are rated "just ok" but at least are delivered with a flourish.

Bayside Brasserie *Continental*

∇ 17 | 14 | 16 | $224

Stanley | 25 Stanley Market Rd. (Stanley Village Rd.) | (852) 2899-0818

"Location, location" is the secret to the success of this breezy Stanley standby whose prime views of the bay make it a favored "Sunday hangout"; its huge, something-for-everyone Continental menu offers dishes from Italian to Indian and just about everything in between, and though the quality is rated "just average", its dining room fills up fast with families on sunny days (arrive early).

Beirut *Mideastern*

19 | 14 | 18 | $247

Lan Kwai Fong | 39 D'Aguilar St. (Lan Kwai Fong) | (852) 2804-6611 | www.beirutbar.com

An oasis of "authentic Lebanese" fare in rowdy Lan Kwai Fong, this "great stop" "hits the spot" with "delicious" shawarma, hummus and "fresh-baked pita" at prices to treat your "wallet right"; it's nothing fancy and can get crowded at prime times, but takeaway is always an option.

Bistro Manchu *Chinese*

∇ 18 | 15 | 18 | $188

Soho | 33 Elgin St. (bet. Peel & Shelley Sts.) | (852) 2536-9218

"In a town full of Cantonese, sometimes you need a bit of the North" declare devotees of this "cozy" Soho Manchurian "favorite" that's particularly beloved for its "hit-the-spot" sauerkraut-pork dumplings and other specialties "hearty enough to put hair on your chest"; "warm" service and prime "people-watching" are other pluses.

Bizou Bistro Cuisine *Californian*

∇ 18 | 16 | 18 | $303

Soho | 49 Elgin St. (Shelley St.) | (852) 2147-0100

A rare source for Californian cuisine in Hong Kong, this "affordable" Soho bistro is known for its home-cooking favorites, like chicken straight from the rotisserie, made with quality ingredients; its appealingly "lively" atmosphere is abetted by the "open-fronted" setup looking out over a "very hip streetscape."

Black Sheep *Eclectic/French*   ▽ 21 | 14 | 20 | $265

Shek O | 350 Shek O Village (Shek O Rd.) | (852) 2809-2021

Urbanites willingly make the "45-minute drive" to "quaint, historic" Shek O in order to visit this "quirky" standout that's "reminiscent of a country pub", but boasts "lovely", sophisticated French-Eclectic cuisine; its "laid-back local atmosphere" keeps "bringing back the regulars", who know to pack a flashlight in order to peruse the menu (lighting is dim); P.S. "take a walk on the beach" before or after eating.

Boathouse, The *Continental*   20 | 20 | 18 | $239

Stanley | 86-88 Stanley Main St. (Stanley Village Rd.) | (852) 2813-4467 | www.igors.com

You can "chow down after a day of shopping at Stanley Market" at this "relaxing" three-story waterside surf 'n' turfer with "alfresco seating on the roof" and "romantic" balcony, both offering "great views" over the bay; though less memorable than the surroundings, the Continental menu is "respectable" ("don't miss the bucket of mixed seafood" for sharing with a group) and the staff is "accommodating to children", plus there's "people-watching" aplenty; P.S. "keep climbing upstairs" for the best vistas.

Boca Tapas & Wine Bar ☻ *Spanish*   20 | 19 | 18 | $258

Soho | 65 Peel St. (Elgin St.) | (852) 2548-1717 | www.boca.com.hk

The "good-looking crowd" downing "tasty" small plates and vino kick up a "lively scene" lasting into the wee hours at this "trendy" Soho Spaniard considered "one of the best tapas bars in town"; critics find the setting "uninspired", but even they can recommend the "front tables looking out onto Peel Street."

Bo Innovation *Asian Fusion/Eclectic*   20 | 16 | 18 | $735

Central | 32-38 Ice House St. (Wyndham St.) | (852) 2850-8371 | www.boinnovation.com

At his Eclectic eatery in Central, chef Alvin Leung (a disciple of the Spanish molecular gastronomy originator Ferran Adrià) demonstrates a "constant desire to surprise his audience" with "unpredictable" flavors and textures "combining Western and Chinese cooking methods and ingredients"; all agree it's a "memorable" experience – with price tags to match – though one diner's "innovative" is another's "weird."

Bombay Dreams *Indian* | 24 | 15 | 18 | $279

Central | Carfield Bldg. | 75-77 Wyndham St. (Pottinger St.) | (852) 2971-0001

A "good value" in the "heart of Central", this moderately priced Indian is the "favorite" of many for its "excellent" lunch and weekend buffets and "individually prepared" dosas; the bright, "casual" setting is "definitely not for a romantic date" and best if you're coming just "to eat, not linger."

NEW Bricolage 62 *Continental* | ▽ 18 | 13 | 17 | $269

Soho | 62 Hollywood Rd. (Elgin St.) | (852) 2542-1991

Tribute's new sibling in Soho is this sleek brasserie serving an "unassuming" but "well-executed" menu of "modern" Continental fare in a "renovated" "historic site" with "interesting" steel-accented decor; cineastes will appreciate the classic films occasionally projected on the wall, but claustrophobes carp about the "tiny" digs and "uncomfortable seating arrangement."

Cafe Deco ❶ *Asian/Continental* | 18 | 20 | 18 | $298

The Peak | Peak Galleria | 118 Peak Rd. | (852) 2849-5650 | www.cafedecogroup.com

"Breathtaking views" of Victoria Harbour make this Asian-Continental sitting "on top of the Peak" a "must-visit for first-timers" and other out-of-towners, especially during fireworks season, while the "cheerful" decor and "cavernous" space are also "geared for tourists"; the service is merely "so-so", though, and foodies advise it's best to "stick with the basics" on a menu that's "all over the place."

Café Landmark *Continental* | 16 | 16 | 14 | $283

Central | The Landmark | 11 Pedder St., 2nd fl. (Queen's Rd. Central) | (852) 2526-4200 | www.maxims.hk

The "ultimate place for *tai tais* (ladies who lunch) and local celebrities", this "open-air" Continental in Central's "chic" Landmark shopping center is a popular, if somewhat "expensive", stop for "brunch", an "easy bite while shopping", "business lunch" or afternoon tea; cynics insist the "prime location" is its only draw, and deem the "no-name food in designer surroundings" a lamentable "waste of space."

	FOOD	DECOR	SERVICE	COST

Café TOO *Eclectic*
23 | 20 | 21 | $367

Admiralty | Island Shangri-La | Pacific Pl. (Supreme Court Rd.) | (852) 2820-8571 | www.shangri-la.com/island

Taking "buffet to another – fabulous – level", this Eclectic in the Admiralty's Island Shangri-La hotel offers a "wide variety" of "well-presented", "world-class" Euro and Asian dishes in a "stylish" space with an open kitchen; the "chic surroundings" and "upmarket" prices notwithstanding, it's "child-friendly" and "good for family celebrations."

☑ Caprice *French*
25 | 27 | 26 | $830

Central | Four Seasons | 8 Finance St. (Connaught Rd.) | (852) 3196-8888 | www.fourseasons.com

"One of the most beautiful" restaurants in Hong Kong is the Four Seasons' French in Central, where you "enter through carved doors" onto a "glass walkway lit from below" and arrive in an "elegant" room with "glorious views" of Victoria Harbour; add "impeccable" service from an "attentive" staff", chef Vincent Thierry's (ex Le Cinq in Paris) "exquisite" Gallic cuisine and an "epic" wine list, and you have a "wonderful", albeit "expensive", place for "special occasions."

Chez Patrick *French*
20 | 20 | 18 | $646

Soho | 22-26 Peel St. (Hollywood Rd.) | (852) 2541-1401 🗷
NEW Star Street | 8-9 Sun St. (Star St.) | (852) 2527-1408
www.chezpatrick.hk

At his Soho establishment, chef Patrick Goubier is a "real character", wont to "charm the ladies with his French accent" and "passionate" about his "authentic", "quality" Gallic cuisine; "stylish" decor and a "comfy setting" make you forget that it's located down the street from 'wet' markets, which sell live animals destined for dinner tables; N.B. the Star Street branch opened in 2007.

Chilli N Spice *Pan-Asian*
19 | 14 | 18 | $195

Sai Wan | The Westwood | 8 Belcher's St., level 1 (Sands St.) | (852) 2542-7777
Stanley | Stanley Plaza | Murray House, Shop 101 (Stanley Main St.) | (852) 2899-0147
www.kingparrot.com

Housed in one of Hong Kong's oldest buildings, the Murray House, which was relocated, brick by brick, from Central to its present Stanley location facing the South China Sea, this Pan-Asian and its Sai Wan sibling offer a "beautiful view" with "decent" Malaysian, Thai and Vietnamese dishes in a "lovely" setting; foodies, though, are unimpressed by the "chainlike sameness" of the fare.

☑ China Club ◑ *Chinese*   22 | 27 | 23 | $516

Central | Old Bank of China Bldg. | Bank St., 13th & 14th fls.
(Queen's Rd. Central) | (852) 2521-8888 | www.chinaclub.com.sg

It's "worth getting to know someone who can get you in" to David Tang's "beautiful", multilevel members-only Chinese in Central, "where the elite go to remind themselves that they are the elite"; a "fantastic", "eclectic" art collection graces the "beautiful" "Shanghai-style" space, where a "quirky but charming" staff entertains a mainly *gweilo* crowd with "acrobatic tea pourings" and more; the menu, which includes dim sum, is "solid and basic", but most agree "you go for the experience."

China Tee Club ☒ *Chinese/Continental*   18 | 20 | 19 | $255

Central | Pedder Bldg. | 12 Pedder St. (Queen's Rd. Central) |
(852) 2521-0233 | www.chinateeclub.com

A "throwback to the English clubs" of yore, this Chinese-Continental in Central is a "lovely place for afternoon tea" or "lunch while shopping" in a "cozy", "colonial" space manned by a "well-trained" staff; the fare is "consistently decent" and many are "impressed by the variety"; N.B. though private, it will take lunch reservations from non-members.

Chinnery, The ☒ *English*   23 | 24 | 26 | $466

Central | Mandarin Oriental | 5 Connaught Rd. (Ice House St.) |
(852) 2522-0111 | www.mandarinoriental.com

"The sun never sets on the British empire" at this "high-end pub" in the Central's Mandarin Oriental, where the "delicious", "traditional English fare" – from fish 'n' chips to Stilton cheese soup – is matched by "quality beers" and a formidable selection of single-malt whiskeys, all served by an "excellent" staff; the room's "rich leather chairs" and banquettes play host to "cozy discussions about business or soccer", as well as to assignations in the 'lovers' corner.'

Chiu Chow Garden *Chinese*   ∇ 21 | 18 | 18 | $149

Central | Jardin House | 1 Connaught Pl. (Man Yiu St.) | (852) 2525-8246 |
www.maxims.hk

"Authentic" poultry- and seafood-centric Chiu Chow cuisine from eastern Guangdong province is served at this sprawling Chinese in

Central that "caters to a wide range of tastes" with "succulent" dishes such as the signature chicken and sliced goose; the "exotic" banquet hall–like space is also a memorable experience for "traveler and resident" alike.

Cinecittà *Italian*

19 | 19 | 17 | $409

Star Street | 9 Star St. (Monmouth Path) | (852) 2529-0199 | www.elite-concepts.com

It's always "Italian movie night" at this "hip", "upscale" Star Street paesano with a cineaste theme in a "hard-to-find" location; it offers a "large menu" of "basic" red-sauce fare, including "quality homemade pastas", and selections from a "great wine list" amid "cool environs" that include a "nice terrace" for alfresco dining.

Ciprani's ⊠ *Italian*

23 | 19 | 23 | $553

Central | Old Bank of China Bldg. | Bank St., 12th fl. (Queen's Rd. Central) | (852) 2501-0222 | www.cipriani.com

"Ladies who lunch abound" at this "expense-account" Italian in Central offering "classic", "reliable" dishes, "wonderful desserts" and "superior" service in "spacious, modern" digs; critics demur at the "dated" decor and "lack of atmosphere", and find it "unjustifiably expensive."

Clipper Lounge *English*

22 | 22 | 25 | $299

Central | Mandarin Oriental | 5 Connaught Rd. (Ice House St.) | (852) 2522-0111 | www.mandarinoriental.com

The "legendary high tea" – complete with "delectable" scones and rose petal jam – "still lives up to its reputation" at this "charming" Central fixture in the recently renovated Mandarin Oriental; "expats" say it's "the old Hong Kong, where deals get made" over "power breakfasts" and "after-work drinks", and the buffet of "comforting" British and Asian fare is "one of the best in town."

Cococabana *French/Mediterranean*

16 | 20 | 13 | $254

Deep Water Bay | Beach Bldg., 2nd fl. | Island Rd. (Sham Sei Wan) | (852) 2812-2226 | www.toptables.com.hk/coco

An "outstanding beachfront location" is the thing at this Deep Water Bay French-Mediterranean standby, which also is known for its impressive, "decent-value" list of rosé wines from France; ok, maybe the service is "slow" and the food "nothing to write home about", but for most the "amazing view and atmosphere" trumps all.

FOOD | DECOR | SERVICE | COST

Cova *Italian*

19 | 20 | 18 | $322

Causeway Bay | Lee Gardens | 33 Hysan Ave. (Yun Ping Rd.) |
(852) 2907-3399 | www.cova.com.hk

An offshoot of the Milan-based pasticceria chain, this lavish Causeway
Bay "find" is "famous for its desserts" and some of the "best coffee in
town", but it also offers a full menu of old-world Italian favorites; it's a
"classy little place" where service is "with a smile."

Craftsteak *Steak*

22 | 21 | 20 | $484

Soho | 29 Elgin St. (Shelley St.) | (852) 2526-0999

Although unrelated to Tom Colicchio's red meateries in the U.S., this
Soho chophouse delivers a "rather American experience" with its "basic"
but "dependable" lineup of "classic steaks" backed by a "decent wine
list" (including plenty of hearty "Aussie reds"); "relaxed service" and
"good desserts" are two more reasons it's something of a crowd-pleaser.

Z Crystal Jade *Chinese*

23 | 14 | 15 | $135

Tsim Sha Tsui | Harbour City | Ocean Terminal, 3rd fl. (Canton Rd.) |
(852) 2622-2699

Fans consider the "knockout" soup dumplings here some of the best
outside of Shanghai, and the handmade noodles are "excellent", so it's
no wonder that this "cheap and cheerful", "no-surprises" Chinese
chain link in Tsim Sha Tsui (voted Hong Kong's Best Buy) attracts "long
lines", especially at lunchtime; the "no-frills" modern decor and "in-and-
out" service suits most fine, especially considering the "value" prices.

Cuisine Cuisine ● *Chinese*

18 | 22 | 18 | $538

Central | IFC Mall | 8 Finance St., 3rd fl. (Connaught Rd.) | (852) 2393-3933 |
www.cuisinecuisine.hk

Perfect for "power lunching" or "impressing" "out-of-town guests"
who "haven't had Cantonese food before", this Central eatery is a
"high-end" source for authentic, "quality" fare; still, connoisseurs contend that despite the name, it's not the food but the "excellent view"
of Victoria Harbour that's "pretty much why you want to dine here."

Da Domenico *Italian*

26 | 14 | 15 | $690

Causeway Bay | Sunning Plaza | 8 Hoi Ping Rd. (Hysan Ave.) |
(852) 2882-8013

"Simple but top-notch" Italian cooking and a "cult"-like following
heavy on "tycoons and celebrities" are the claim to fame of this

	FOOD	DECOR	SERVICE	COST

Causeway Bay scenester; everything down to the salt is "freshly flown in" from Italy – a mark of "authenticity" that's reflected in its "astronomical" prices – and while the "small" quarters are decidedly "down-to-earth" and the service "limited", nothing seems to stifle its "snob appeal."

Dan Ryan's Chicago Grill *American*

| 16 | 14 | 16 | $229 |

Admiralty | Pacific Pl. | 88 Queensway, 2nd fl. (Queen's Rd. Central) | (852) 2845-4600 | www.danryans.com

Homesick expats take "quick trips back home" via this Admiralty chophouse known for its burgers, steaks and other "American-style" basics in "large portions"; a "watering hole" perfect for watching "ball games back in the States" over a frosty Bud, it's also "great for families" given the "crayons, balloons" and "kid-friendly" staff – though, no surprise, it "can get noisy" at prime times.

Da Ping Huo *Chinese*

| 24 | 19 | 22 | $309 |

Soho | 49 Hollywood Rd. (Graham St.) | (852) 2559-1317

"Thumbs-up" for "real" "burn-your-tongue Sichuan" cheer connoisseurs of the "spectacularly spicy" specialties of this Soho "hot" spot; in addition to the "kick-ass" cuisine, a "cool", "arty" vibe and postmeal performances from the "chef-cum–opera singer" make for overall "unique experiences" here; N.B. it's BYO.

Dim Sum The Art of Chinese Tidbits ◐ *Chinese*

| 25 | 15 | 20 | $227 |

Happy Valley | 63 Sing Woo Rd. (Shing Ping St.) | (852) 2834-8893

"Dim sum elevated to an art form" is the deal at this "tiny", no-frills Happy Valley standout that's a rare "24-hour" source for "fantastic", "quality" tidbits the likes of dumplings with shark fin or shu mai with gold leaf; it's "*gweilo*-friendly" (i.e. "English menu with pictures") and "has been discovered by everyone", so "come at off times to avoid long waits."

Dirty Duck Diner *SE Asian*

| - | - | - | M |

Wan Chai | The Broadway | 54-62 Lockhart Rd. (Fenwick St.) | (852) 2217-8000 | www.elite-concepts.com

"Book a booth on the balcony in mild weather" and feel like you're in Bali at this Wan Chai Asian most appreciated for its atmospheric "great outdoor seating area" featuring low teak tables and colorful floor cushions; however, the Indonesian eats are deemed merely "decent", though the house-specialty "crispy fried duck" is a standout.

Di Vino 🛇 *Italian*

23 | 23 | 21 | $304

Central | 73 Wyndham St. (Pottinger St.) | (852) 2167-8883 | www.divino.com.hk

Jet-setting over-30 types collect at this Central sophisticate, located right outside Lan Kwai Fong, offering a "wide-ranging" menu of Italian dishes "impeccably served" and what may be "one of the largest wine lists in Hong Kong"; it's got "great buzz" and a certain "NY feeling about it", leading many to favor it for after-work drinks or late-night bites.

Dong Lai Shun *Chinese/Mongolian*

- | - | - | VE

Tsim Sha Tsui | The Royal Garden | 69 Mody Rd. (Mody Ln.) | (852) 2733-2020 | www.rghk.com.hk

Specializing in Beijing and Huaiyang cuisine, this Tsim Sha Tsui hotel eatery is known for its mutton hot pot, seasonal crab dishes and other "great food with an Islamic bent"; however, it's more the elegant, old-world decor that draws its beautiful-people clientele, which shrugs "who cares" when it comes to the "expensive" tab.

Dot Cod Seafood Restaurant & Oyster Bar *English/Seafood*

19 | 14 | 18 | $422

Central | Prince's Bldg. | 10 Chater Rd. (Queen's Rd. Central) | (852) 2810-6988

A "sea of suits" fills this Central seafooder for "better-than-expected" (if "not terribly exciting") fish 'n' chips and other standards delivered by a "crisp", "friendly" staff; at lunchtime its "sedate" setting is "perfect for serious discussions", but keep in mind that happy hour starts early here with "power stockbroker" types stopping by for "after-work beers."

Dozo! *Japanese*

13 | 15 | 12 | $250

Soho | 44 Lyndhurst Terrace (Wyndham St.) | (852) 2581-1338 | www.dozosushi.com

"Sushi with a contemporary twist" is the deal at this "trendy" Soho Japanese where the rolls are delivered via conveyor belt and the "hip", clublike atmosphere is big "fun"; critics citing "fast food–type" quality and "patchy service" call it "mediocre", but even they plug the "entertaining people-watching" afforded by its Lyndhurst Terrace view.

DINING

	FOOD	DECOR	SERVICE	COST

Dragon-I *Chinese/Japanese*   18 | 24 | 17 | $364

Central | 60 Wyndham St. (D'Aguilar St.) | (852) 3110-1222 |
www.dragon-i.com.hk

Famous as a "model hangout"/"see-and-be-seen" scene complete
with "velvet rope", this "gorgeous", "ultraglam" Central destination is widely favored "for the people-watching, not the food" (a
pricey mix of Chinese and Japanese dishes); however, those not in the
"supermodel or rock star" category tout the "more affordable" dim
sum lunch, best enjoyed out on the "impressive" terrace hung with
cages of songbirds.

Fai Seafood Hot Pot ◐ *Chinese*   – | – | – | E

Kowloon City | Full Sing Court | 82-84 Fuk Lo Tsun Rd. (Carpenter Rd.) |
(852) 2382-2000

A family magnet at the dinner hour and a celebrity hangout late-night,
this "hole-in-the-wall" traditional Chinese banquet house in Kowloon
is known for, yes, "delicious" seafood hot pot dishes; it's "an experience" that devotees say "won't disappoint" – just "bring your appe-
tite" and a stack of cash (prices tend toward the "high-end").

Farm House *Chinese*   23 | 14 | 18 | $355

Causeway Bay | AIA Plaza | 18 Hysan Ave. (Yun Ping Rd.) | (852) 2881-1331 |
www.farmhouse.com.hk

Among the "innovative", mostly MSG-free specialties at this unpretentious Causeway Bay Cantonese eatery are "unbelievable" sticky
rice–stuffed chicken wings that smitten surveyors say are "not to be
missed"; though some are unimpressed with the service, regulars re-
port "known customers get better" treatment.

🅉 Felix ◐ *Continental*   21 | 27 | 23 | $606

Tsim Sha Tsui | The Peninsula | Salisbury Rd., 28th fl. (Nathan Rd.) |
(852) 2315-3188 | www.hongkong.peninsula.com

Philippe Starck makes his way to Hong Kong via this "lavish" "hipster"
(voted Hong Kong's Most Popular restaurant) atop Tsim Sha Tsui's
Peninsula hotel, where "jaw-dropping" 360-degree vistas of the harbor and city skyline meet "sexy" modern design with "stunning"
results – and prices to match; maybe it's mostly about the "over-the-
top atmosphere" and "beautiful-people" crowd here, but those who
can focus on the Continental cuisine say it's "delicious"; N.B. "don't

forget to check out" the "spectacular" men's WC, as well as the "must-visit" upstairs bar.

FINDS ● *Scandinavian* | 17 | 22 | 20 | $447 |

Lan Kwai Fong | LKF Tower | 33 Wyndham St., 2nd fl. (D'Aguilar St.) | (852) 2522-9318 | www.finds.com.hk

One of Hong Kong's only sources for Scandinavian, this "trendy" Lan Kwai Fong "hipster" thrives more on the power of its "so-o cool" icy-blue lounge and expert cocktails than its "interesting" fare; it's no surprise, then, that it becomes more "like a club later on weekends", with "borderline-oppressive noise levels", but to fans that's part of the "fun."

Fish Bar *Seafood* | 20 | 18 | 20 | $332 |

Admiralty | JW Marriott | 88 Queensway, 7th fl. (Queen's Rd. Central) | (852) 2841-3858 | www.jwmarriotthk.com

"Surprisingly located" beside the pool at the JW Marriott in Admiralty, this "relaxed" seafooder's "alfresco" meals feature "simple" fish preparations ("deep-fried, pan-fried", etc.) ordered from a chalkboard menu; something of a "well-kept secret", it makes for a "nice change of pace", so long as "it's not blazing hot" out.

☑ Fook Lam Moon Restaurant *Chinese* | 26 | 16 | 21 | $518 |

Wan Chai | Newman House | 35-45 Johnston Rd. (Luard Rd.) | (852) 2866-0633 | www.fooklammoon-grp.com

"Some of the best Cantonese food you can find in Hong Kong" comes out of the kitchen of this "old-school" Wan Chai institution known for its "to-die-for dim sum" and luxury specialties ("shark's fin soup, abalone", etc.); "upscale" prices and a "tycoon and *tai tai*-heavy clientele have earned it the nickname the "millionaire's canteen", where "you must go with a regular" or service "can be lacking", but still to most it "doesn't get much better than this."

Frog Faced Fish *Seafood* | 16 | 15 | 17 | $400 |

Central | 43-55 Wyndham St. (bet. Arbuthnot & Lower Albert Rds.) | (852) 2869-8535 | www.frogfacefish.com

Moored on a "now-trendy" Wyndham Street party block, this seafooder's strongest lure may be the "wonderful people-watching" afforded by its "big windows to the busy street" outside; as for the fin fare, most rate it "decent", if "not inspiring or memorable", though the three-course lunch set menu for under $100 is an undeniable bargain.

⛿ Gaddi's *French* | 27 | 26 | 29 | $769 |

Tsim Sha Tsui | The Peninsula | Salisbury Rd. (Nathan Rd.) | (852) 2315-3171 | www.hongkong.peninsula.com

"Time stands still" (in a good way) at this "old-world", chandelier-bedecked "jewel box" in Tsim Sha Tsui's Peninsula hotel, a "European palatial"–style "landmark" that's "as fancy and classically French as can be found in Hong Kong"; the "world-class" fare and decor are surpassed only by the near-"perfect" "formal" service (Hong Kong's No. 1 in this Survey), and while such "not-to-be-missed" experiences come at a "stiff price", the "rich-and-famous" types who dine here swear it's "worth every cent"; P.S. for "extraordinarily special occasions", book the chef's table in the kitchen.

Gaia Ristorante ⬤ *Italian* | 25 | 23 | 23 | $576 |

Sheung Wan | Grand Millennium Plaza | 181 Queen's Rd. Central (Wing Wo St.) | (852) 2167-8200 | www.gaiaristorante.com

This "romantic" Italian "sanctuary" in a "quiet" corner of Sheung Wan is beloved for its "verdant" "outdoor terrace" complete with gurgling fountain, a fitting backdrop for its "simple" yet "divine" (and "expensive") dishes paired with "well-selected" wines; inside, its "dramatic" quarters are ruby-plush and offer a plethora of semi-private rooms, making it ideal for first dates as well as "special occasions and business dinners."

Gaylord *Indian* | - | - | - | M |

Tsim Sha Tsui | 23-25 Ashley Rd., 1st fl. (Peking Rd.) | (852) 2376-1001

Look past the name to find this venerable North Indian at Tsim Sha Tsui's Ashley Center cooking up curries since 1972; while low lighting, comfortable booths and nightly live music enhance the swank setting, it's the classic, authentic fare that keeps it popular with the local Indian community, expats and visitors alike, even if you may pay more here than you would elsewhere.

Gough 40 Cafe ⬤⊄ *Continental/French* | - | - | - | VE |

Sheung Wan | 40 Gough St. (Shin Hing St.) | (852) 2851-8498

Parked on a "road reminiscent of a French cul de sac" in an out-of-the-way corner of Sheung Wan, this tiny (30 seats), all-white jewel box is "worth a detour" according to fans for its Gallic-Continental cuisine served with "no pretentiousness", despite the high-end prices; its "casual" "local" ambiance becomes all the more appealing when, on a nice evening, they open the French doors to serve out on the sidewalk.

Green T. House ● *Chinese* ▽ 17 | 15 | 18 | $298

Cyberport | The Arcade | 100 Cyberport Rd. (Information Crescent) | (852) 2989-6036 | www.green-t-house.com

Imagine dining on the set of *2001: A Space Odyssey* and you've got this "super-trendy" eatery set in a Cyberport shopping center, whose "over-the-top", all-white dining room is accented with neon lighting and seven-ft. high-back chairs; as for the "Chinese-with-a-twist" cuisine featuring "dishes with fancy names that sound more like artwork than food" (many made with green tea), some say "delicious" and others simply "bizarre."

Grill at Plateau, The ● *Continental* - | - | - | VE

Wan Chai | Grand Hyatt | 1 Harbour Rd. (Convention Ave.) | (852) 2588-1234 | www.hongkong.grand.hyatt.com

When the weather is clear, expect a full house, which may include a number of celebs, at this hotel Continental in Wan Chai offering poolside dining and drop-dead views of Victoria Harbour in a "super-relaxed" atmosphere; the BBQ dinner buffet featuring steak and fancy seafood and incredible dessert bar are a relative "bargain", and the service is "what you expect to get at a Grand Hyatt."

Grissini *Italian* 23 | 22 | 23 | $604

Wan Chai | Grand Hyatt | 1 Harbour Rd., 2nd fl. (Convention Ave.) | (852) 2588-7933 | www.hongkong.grand.hyatt.com

Known for its "best-in-town" namesake crispy breadsticks, this "high-end" Wan Chai Italian inside the Grand Hyatt hotel is also appreciated for its "top-notch", "authentic" cuisine, "notable" service and "fabulous" setting boasting a "wonderful view of the harbor"; true, it costs "an awful lot", but the standout Boot-centric vino list alone keeps oenophiles "coming again and again."

Habibi *African* 19 | 16 | 15 | $274

Central | 112-114 Wellington St. (Gutzlaff St.) | (852) 2544-3886 | www.habibi.com.hk

"Worth a try" for a "change of pace", this " "cheap-and-cheerful" Central Egyptian is known especially for its "outstanding dips" and other meze that are the beginning of a "hearty" "traditional" meal; the "laid-back" atmosphere is enhanced with pillows, tented fabric and even occasional entertainment from "cool belly dancers."

Habitu The Garden *Italian*
Causeway Bay | Lee Gardens Two | 28 Yun Ping Rd., 3rd fl. (Hysan Ave.) | (852) 2989-3919

| 14 | 19 | 14 | $312 |

Never mind the moniker – this Causeway Bay Italian no longer offers alfresco seating, but it does boast an "airy", "spacious" dining room reminiscent of a ship's interior; it's "nothing fancy" and some find the "basic" pizzas, pastas and such to be just "so-so", but all the same many rely on it as a "tasteful" fallback for a "casual" bite.

Harlan's *American*
Central | IFC Mall | 8 Finance St., 2nd fl. (Connaught Rd.) | (852) 2805-0566 | www.harlang.com

| 20 | 19 | 19 | $639 |

A favorite "place to be seen", especially among the banker set, this sleek, modern Central steak-centric American from chef Harlan Goldstein is considered a "must" for "good", "often innovative" fare; skeptics decry the "sky-high prices" and wonder "what's all the rave about?" – but even they concede the "amazing" harbor views are hard to beat.

ⓩ Hutong ◑ *Chinese*
Tsim Sha Tsui | One Peking Rd. | 1 Peking Rd., 28th fl. (Kowloon Park Dr.) | (852) 3428-8342

| 24 | 28 | 21 | $578 |

"It's easy to forget you're at the top of one of Hong Kong's most modern skyscrapers" when you dine at this "high-end" Tsim Sha Tsui Chinese, whose "wonderful", "antiques-filled" space evokes "old Beijing" – "astounding" Victoria Harbour vistas notwithstanding; yes, most "go here for the view", but the "intriguing" cuisine is declared "excellent" as well – though be warned that among its specialties are some "mind-numbingly spicy" dishes.

Imasa *Japanese*
Tsim Sha Tsui | The Peninsula | Salisbury Rd. (Nathan Rd.) | (852) 2315-3175 | www.hongkong.peninsula.com

| - | - | - | VE |

Set in the Peninsula hotel, this luxe Tsim Sha Tsui Japanese specializes in impeccable, jet-fresh sushi and other traditional specialties like shabu-shabu, sukiyaki, sashimi and stone-grilled dishes; the contemporary Zen-like dining room is manned by a highly professional crew; N.B. it also has two private dining rooms.

	FOOD	DECOR	SERVICE	COST

Inagiku *Japanese*

25 | 24 | 23 | $640

NEW **Central** | Four Seasons | 8 Finance St., 4th fl. (Connaught Rd.) | (852) 2805-0600 | www.fourseasons.com
Tsim Sha Tsui | The Royal Garden | 69 Mody Rd., 1st fl. (Mody Ln.) | (852) 2733-2933 | www.rghk.com.hk

Considered an all-around "class" act, this upscale hotel Japanese duo specializes in teppanyaki dishes and "lighter-than-air" tempura, but it also boasts a sushi bar offering "fresh, varied" takes on the genre; it's admired nearly as much for its "cool" decor and "wonderful" staff as for its "excellent" cuisine, and though the experience will cost you, most maintain "you get what you pay for."

Indochine 1929 *Vietnamese*

22 | 20 | 20 | $374

Lan Kwai Fong | California Tower | 30-32 D'Aguilar St. (Lan Kwai Fong) | (852) 2869-7399

A "French colonial–themed oasis" above the "Lan Kwai Fong throng", this Vietnamese is just the thing for a "low-key date" or a "relaxing" dinner "with friends"; the "enjoyable" fare is "a little pricey", but most don't mind much considering "wonderful ambiance" and the "great" service.

Indonesian Restaurant 1968 ● *Indonesian* (aka IR 1968)

19 | 14 | 13 | $173

Causeway Bay | 28 Leighton Rd. (Percival St.) | (852) 2577-9981 | www.indonesianrestaurant1968.com

The "authentic, delicious" fare hasn't changed much since this Causeway Bay Indonesian opened in 1968, but thanks to a recent redo it's now served in a "contemporary, minimalist" setting; the staff at this "best-kept little secret" can be on the "slow" side, but most don't mind much considering the "reasonable" prices.

Ingredients *Continental*

16 | 19 | 16 | $561

Star Street | 23 Wing Fung St. (Star St.) | (852) 2544-5133 | www.ingredients.com.hk

Once a "modest" "little private kitchen", this Continental eatery has relocated to "cool" Star Street and "blossomed" into a "chic" tri-level affair featuring a formal dining room, a jazz/oyster bar and a rooftop patio; all agree the "decor is much nicer in the new setting", but nostalgists who "long for the old days" find the fare and service just "so-so" and lament the "get-your-bank-manager-to-take-you" prices.

	FOOD	DECOR	SERVICE	COST

Isola Bar & Grill *Italian*

| 22 | 24 | 19 | $493 |

Central | IFC Mall | 8 Finance St., 3rd fl. (Connaught Rd.) | (852) 2383-8765 | www.isolabarandgrill.com

On the waterfront at the IFC Mall, this "trendy" Italian offers some of the "best terrace dining in Hong Kong" given its "superb" views out over Victoria Harbour – but its sleek, "all-white" interior has a "great ambiance" as well; the kitchen's "simple" yet "stylish" handiwork is considered "delicious", and especially popular at weekend brunch (reservations are a "must").

Jaspa's ● *Continental*

| 18 | 14 | 18 | $302 |

Soho | 28 Staunton St. (Graham St.) | (852) 2869-0733

"Consistency is the hallmark" of this family-friendly Soho "staple" that "can always be relied on" to dish up Continental "comfort food" in portions that "rival those of the U.S."; even if the eats are "not always inspired", the "mostly Western crowd" doesn't seem to mind and neither do others who flock here for "relaxed" casual dining and the "pleasant" weekend brunch.

Jimmy's Kitchen *Continental*

| 20 | 17 | 22 | $332 |

Central | 1-3 Wyndham St. (Queen's Rd. Central) | (852) 2526-5293
Tsim Sha Tsui | Kowloon Ctr. | 29 Ashley Rd., ground fl. (bet. Haiphong & Peking Rds.) | (852) 2376-0327
www.jimmys.com

After eight decades, these "classic" "throwbacks" to Hong Kong are still kicking thanks to an "outstanding" staff and an "extensive" Continental menu, running the gamut from steaks to Indian curries, that'll induce "cravings in the future"; the duo may be a "bit worn at the elbows" and the "sub-ground" setting in Central isn't for everyone, but most agree these "institutions" are a "must visit"; N.B. the Tsim Sha Tsui branch's post-Survey relocation to a new space in the Kowloon Centre is not reflected in the Decor score.

Jumbo Floating Restaurant *Chinese/Seafood*
(aka Jumbo Kingdom)

| 16 | 18 | 16 | $336 |

Wong Chuk Hang | Shum Pier Dr. (bet. Nam Long Shan & Welfare Rds.) | (852) 2553-9111 | www.jumbokingdom.com

"What a hoot!" cheer "first-timers" for this Wong Chuk Hang "tourist icon" that seems like the "world's largest" floating restaurant right in

Aberdeen Harbor; "Westernized" Cantonese and "mediocre" seafood come with "expensive" tabs but "it's worth going for the experience anyway", so "bring your camera" for the "many photo ops" to be had amid the "gaudy" gold decor and tanks brimming with "live fish in the back" – "you'd be remiss to not go once."

Kaya Korean Restaurant Korean

▽ 19 | 13 | 15 | $263

Causeway Bay | 8 Russell St., 6th fl. (Percival St.) | (852) 2838-9550

"Authentic" Korean fare and an "affordable" lunch menu attract those seeking respite from the bustle of Causeway Bay at this open, comfortable grill that comes "without the hokey Korean BBQ atmosphere"; grab a cushioned booth by the windows overlooking Times Square for prime people-watching.

Kee Club ⊠ Continental

20 | 23 | 23 | $640

Lan Kwai Fong | 32 Wellington St., 6th fl. (D'Aguilar St.) | (852) 2810-9000 | www.keeclub.com

Catering to a "glam crowd of expats and local socialites", this "intimate" Lan Kwai Fong private club delivers "innovative" Continental cuisine amid lush surroundings, where you can explore the art hidden in tiny offshoot rooms like the library, and even if you'll "have trouble seeing what you're eating" (after all, it's "first and foremost a bar and club"), it's "an amazing place – if you can afford it!"; N.B. jackets suggested.

Kenjo's Japanese

▽ 29 | 10 | 17 | $764

Tsim Sha Tsui | 30 Minden Ave. (Minden Row) | (852) 2369-8307

Elbow your way into this "hole-in-the-wall" to experience chef Kenjo's "first-class" Japanese fare in Tsim Sha Tsui; the sushi is "superbly fresh" and available through set lunches that are a comparative "bargain" to the usual "pricey" plates on offer, so book ahead and don't be surprised if you find yourself crossing chopsticks with a celeb or CEO – they all eat here.

Kin's Kitchen Chinese

▽ 22 | 14 | 21 | $247

North Point | 9 Tsing Fung St. (Electric Rd.) | (852) 2571-0913

When you're ready to graduate from General Tso's chicken, visit this true to tradition but "innovative" Cantonese in North Point; the "deliberately Western" decor may feel a bit "contrived" (read: poetry-etched glass wall panels) but the "homey" dishes prepared with "fresh" ingredients make up for what they may lack in ambiance.

NEW La Mer Brasserie *French/Seafood*

− | − | − | VE

Lan Kwai Fong | LKF Tower | 33 Wyndham St., 2nd fl. (D'Aguilar St.) | (852) 2523-0200

Sate your seafood cravings at this cavernous art deco space in the LKF Tower where fruits de la mer share the spotlight with seasonal French fare; tuck into a quiet corner in the "large" but "comfortable" room or reserve a table on the terrace overlooking busy Wyndham Street – just don't miss the raw bar where you can pick out what you'd like on your plate later.

Z NEW L'Atelier de Joël Robuchon *French*

27 | 27 | 26 | $984

Central | The Landmark | 11 Pedder St., 4th fl. (Queen's Rd. Central) | (852) 2166-9000 | www.joel-robuchon.com

"Spend your children's inheritance" for a "fabulous experience" at this Robuchon production in Central, where you "sit at the counter and watch the show" unfold in the open kitchen, which produces a tasting menu of "superbly executed", "modern" French cuisine in "small portions", paired with one of the "best wine lists in town"; "beautiful, yet subdued" decor graces the "impressive" space, and the service is "excellent."

Lei Garden *Chinese*

24 | 18 | 20 | $318

Central | IFC Mall | 8 Finance St., 3rd fl. (Man Yiu St.) | (852) 2295-0238

Kowloon City | APM Millenium City 5 | Kwun Tong Rd. (bet. Hoi Yuen Rd. & Tsun Yip St.) | (852) 2365 3238

Mongkok | 121 Sai Yee St. (Fife St.) | (852) 2392-5184

North Point | 9-10 City Garden Rd. (Power St.) | (852) 2806-0008

Tsim Sha Tsui | Houston Ctr., B-2 | 63 Mody Rd. (bet. Chatham Rd. S. & Mody Ln.) | (852) 2722-1636

Wan Chai | CNT Tower | 338 Hennessy Rd., 1st fl. (Morrison Hill Rd.) | (852) 2892-0333

www.leigardenrestaurant.com

A "mostly local" crowd gravitates to this long-standing Chinese chain for "super", "fresh" fare that "rarely surprises", including dim sum that's "worth the one-hour wait for a table"; the "decor varies by location", from the "serene, oh-so-civilized" branch in Central's IFC mall to the Wan Chai location that could use a "revamp."

	FOOD	DECOR	SERVICE	COST

NEW Lian *Thai/Vietnamese*　　　**20** **21** **15** **$280**

Central | IFC Mall | 8 Finance St., 2nd fl. (Connaught Rd.) | (852) 2521-1117 | www.maxims.hk

An "interesting" combination of Thai and Vietnamese dishes keeps this "surprisingly stylish" spot in Central's IFC "packed during lunch" on weekdays; the contemporary space is "bright and airy" and the service is "solid", and while some find it a bit "pricey for a mall restaurant", to others it's a lifeline in a "sea of intimidatingly expensive options."

Life Café *Health Food*　　　**▽ 15** **16** **15** **$258**

Soho | 10 Shelley St. (bet. Hollywood Rd. & Staunton St.) | (852) 2810-9777 | www.lifecafe.com.hk

A rare purveyor of health food in the perfumed port, this Soho special-ist serves "divine" salads and other body-friendly offerings emphasiz-ing organic ingredients, including a number of vegan and gluten-free dishes; some skeptics are cool to the "hit-or-miss" menu, but most en-joy the "chill" atmosphere in the inviting hippie setting.

Little Sheep ● *Mongolian*　　　**22** **12** **13** **$207**

Causeway Bay | Causeway Plaza Two | 463-483 Lockhart Rd. (bet. Canal Rd. Flyover & Percival St.) | (852) 2893-8318
Mongkok | 16 Argyle St. (Portland St.) | (852) 2396-8816
Tseun Wan | City Landmark 1, 5th fl. | 68 Chung On St. (Hoi Pa St.) | (852) 2940-7678
Tsim Sha Tsui | 26 Kimberley Rd. (Carnarvon Rd.) | (852) 2722-7633

For some of the "best selection of lamb" around, fans tout these bright, bustling Mongolian spots that are especially popular in the "winter months" thanks to its signature hot pot, which comes with a variety of ingredients to "please everyone"; the "food and service are as good as you can be", since "you are (your own) cook and waiter."

Z Lobby at Peninsula *Eclectic/English*　　　**22** **27** **26** **$305**

Tsim Sha Tsui | The Peninsula | Salisbury Rd. (Nathan Rd.) | (852) 2315-3171 | www.hongkong.peninsula.com

A "must-do" for visitors is the "spectacular" afternoon tea at this Eclectic-English in the lobby of the Peninsula in Tsim Sha Tsui where "elegant" "old-world" decor "brings back the days" of "Rule Britannia", "starched waiters" provide "impeccable" service and the "fresh" fare is "almost up to par", although the prices might even "make the Queen look twice"; unless you're a hotel guest, you can expect to stand in a "kilometer-long touristy queue" too, but for many the experience and "delectable people-watching" are worth it.

Luk Yu Tea House *Chinese*
20 | 18 | 14 | $219

Central | 24-26 Stanley St. (D'Aguilar St.) | (852) 2523-1970

It's "old-school all the way" at this "ancient dim sum palace" in Central, a local "institution" serving "authentic" Cantonese bites and "traditional" dishes in a "classic" art deco-style "teahouse" setting complete with "spittoons"; though there's English on the menu, there's "little spoken" by the "cranky" staff that "doesn't like non-locals", but aficionados insist the "haphazard" service "only adds to the ambiance."

Lumiere *Chinese*
18 | 25 | 17 | $429

Central | IFC Mall | 8 Finance St., 3rd fl. (Connaught Rd.) | (852) 2393-3933 | www.lumiere.hk

"Spectacular views" of Victoria Harbour from 20-ft.-tall windows and a "beautiful", large modern interior with sexy red lighting make this high-end Chinese a "nice place to bring a date" and a "real treat in the IFC" mall; the "unique", South American–accented Sichuan cuisine features "unusual combinations of flavors", but purists feel the fusion concept is "taken a little too far", while others grouse about the "overpriced" "small portions."

⚡ Lung King Heen *Chinese*
28 | 24 | 24 | $495

Central | Four Seasons | 8 Finance St. (Connaught Rd.) | (852) 3196-8888 | www.fourseasons.com

"Everything from the menu is well executed" at this Chinese housed in the Four Seasons hotel in Central (voted Hong Kong's No. 1 for Food), where "innovative", "top-notch" Cantonese cuisine and an "excellent selection" of "scrumptious" dim sum are paired with an eclectic, China-centric wine list, while "amazing views of the harbor" serve as a backdrop to the "pretty", contemporary room accented with silver and glass; it's "expensive", but the consensus is that the experience is "worth it."

Magnolia Ⓜ➪ *Cajun/Southern*
▽ 25 | 21 | 23 | $367

Sheung Wan | 17 Po Yan St. (Hollywood Rd.) | (852) 2530-9880 | www.magnolia.hk

Owned and operated by "New Orleans transplant" and "Hong Kong legend" Lori Granito, this upscale Cajun "private kitchen" in the "undiscovered neighborhood" of Sheung Wan is a "unique experience", serving "authentic" "Southern comfort food" "family-style" at a communal table with "fantastic" ambiance; the staff is "flexible", and "BYOB makes it a tad cheaper"; N.B. reservations required.

Mandarin Grill & Bar *Eclectic*

| 25 | 24 | 27 | $567 |

Central | Mandarin Oriental | 5 Connaught Rd. (Ice House St.) | (852) 2522-0111 | www.mandarinoriental.com

A "sure winner every time", this "newly renovated", "expense-account" Eclectic in Central's Mandarin Oriental is a "class act", where the "attentive" staff has "everything down pat" and the kitchen turns out "excellent" fare, including the "freshest sashimi and oysters"; the "addition of windows was a tremendous improvement" to the "classic", "elegant" dining room, although a few prefer the old "formal club" setting to the present "glass, chrome and marble" look.

Man Wah *Chinese*

| 26 | 24 | 26 | $528 |

Central | Mandarin Oriental | 5 Connaught Rd. (Ice House St.) | (852) 2522-0111 | www.mandarinoriental.com

"Still worth a visit" after more than 40 years, this "old standby" in the Mandarin Oriental in Central delivers "superb" "traditional" Cantonese cuisine and "excellent" service in an "elegant" room with a "spectacular view of the harbor"; while a few fault the chef for "unimaginative" cooking, it's the "favorite" "upmarket Chinese" of many others.

M at the Fringe *French/Mediterranean*

| 24 | 23 | 24 | $567 |

Central | 2 Lower Albert Rd. (Wyndham St.) | (852) 2877-4000 | www.m-atthefringe.com

Fans "go out of their way" to enjoy this long-standing "gem" located above the Fringe club, an art and performance space in Central, for a "romantic meal with your special someone (or someone else)"; with "wonderful" French-Med cuisine, including "superb" suckling pig, a "fabulous" wine list, "subtle, refined" service and a "très stylish" space, it "always lives up to expectations" and is "always quite full."

Maxim's City Hall *Chinese*

| 22 | 14 | 15 | $173 |

Central | City Hall | Low Block, 2nd fl. (Edinburgh Pl.) | (852) 2521-1303 | www.maxims.hk

"Out-of-town visitors" and locals alike "love the carts pushed around by ladies" at this "cheap and lively" "classic dim sum experience" in

FOOD | DECOR | SERVICE | COST

Central, where a "fantastic selection" of "authentic" Cantonese small bites is "served the original way", against a backdrop of "awesome" harbor views; though the space can seat 500, it's "always full" and regulars recommend "queue up early", for "they don't take reservations."

McSorley's Ale House *Irish*

`11` `13` `11` `$152`

Lantau Island | Discovery Bay Plaza | G11A-1, Block B (Plaza Ln.) | (852) 2987-8280
Soho | 55 Elgin St. (Old Bailey St.) | (852) 2522-2646
www.mcsorleys.com.hk

"Expats abound" at this Irish pub pair offering a "quick escape to the West", with "lots of TVs" for watching sports over burgers and pints and other "good grub", and an upstairs space at the Soho branch that resembles an old NY speakeasy; detractors deride them as "cheap imitations" that "could be found most anywhere – except the U.K."; N.B. the Discovery Bay location offers a children's menu.

Mi-Ne Sushi ● *Japanese*

▽ `18` `13` `14` `$145`

Causeway Bay | 12 Pak Sha Rd. (Yun Ping Rd.) | (852) 3188-2400 | www.minesushi.com

For a "quick sushi fix" that's "surprisingly cheap", fans tout this Causeway Bay *kaiten* (conveyor-belt) sushi spot offering "fresh" fin fare on a "merry-go-round"; the service is "fast" and "friendly" but the "lines are always long" and "no reservations are accepted"; still, "for the price you pay", few find reason to complain.

Modern China *Chinese*

`-` `-` `-` `M`

Causeway Bay | Times Sq. | 1 Matheson St., 10th fl. (Russell St.) | (852) 2506-2525

While the only thing modern about this Causeway Bay Chinese may be its location in Causeway Bay's bustling Times Square mall, traditionalists nonetheless find the Shanghainese fare "fantastic", while the dimly lit, antiques-accoutred setting is "good for business meetings" or entertaining the "parents"; just be "prepared to stand in long lines."

Morton's of Chicago *Steak*

`26` `22` `25` `$592`

Tsim Sha Tsui | Sheraton | 20 Nathan Rd. (Salisbury Rd.) | (852) 2732-2343 | www.mortons.com

For a "taste of America" in Tsim Sha Tsui, carnivores commend this outpost of the chophouse chain in the Sheraton that cronies contend is a "step above most locations in the U.S.", thanks to "excellent" steaks, a "well-balanced wine list" and "prompt", "professional" service; the "clubby, sophisticated" setting and a "first-class view of the skyline" are "icing on the cake", and though the tabs are "hefty", many feel it's "worth it."

Mozart Stub'n 🗲 *Austrian* — ∇ 20 | 15 | 20 | $444

Central | 8 Glenealy Rd. (Wyndham St.) | (852) 2522-1763 | www.mozartstubn.com

Seems like this Austrian in Central "has been around forever", serving "authentic", "reliable" *essen und trinken* in a "dark" setting that's the "definition of cozy", though some feel the decor "could be improved"; it's "tucked away" in a location that's "hard to find", but to those who do, it "feels like a home away from home."

Nadaman *Japanese* — 26 | 20 | 25 | $687

Admiralty | Island Shangri-La | Pacific Pl., 7th fl. (Supreme Court Rd.) | (852) 2820-8570 | www.shangri-la.com/island

A crowd of mostly "old-money" and "business clientele" gravitates to this "fabulous", "pricey" outpost of a venerable Tokyo-based Japanese chain in Admiralty's Island Shangri-La hotel for "amazing", "masterful" kaiseki courses, including "excellent" Wagyu beef, and "impeccable" service; the space, a modern take on "traditional" decor from Japan, includes sushi and teppanyaki counters and a private tatami room.

New Dynasty Scenic *Chinese* — - | - | - | E

Wan Chai | Hopewell Ctr. | 183 Queen's Rd., 60th fl. (Spring Garden Ln.) | (852) 2152-1282

Dazzling 360-degree views from the 60th floor of the Hopewell Centre in Wan Chai give this veteran Cantonese its name, while traditional dim sum at lunch and seafood from live tanks at "decent prices" make it a popular option for families and large parties, even if the space is a "bit cramped"; though the staff's "ability to communicate in English" might be limited, there is a *gweilo*-friendly menu available.

Nha Trang Vietnamese *Vietnamese* — 22 | 11 | 11 | $156

Central | 88-90 Wellington St. (Shelley St.) | (852) 2581-9992

"Huge" helpings of "no-nonsense" pho and other "high-quality" Vietnamese victuals at "reasonable prices" make this Central spot on bustling Wellington Street "extremely popular"; the digs are "cramped"

	FOOD	DECOR	SERVICE	COST

and "no place to linger", especially during peak times when the "rude" staff is "eager to chase you out", but for "great value" most agree it's a "sure winner."

Nicholini's *Italian*   23 | 20 | 24 | $568

Admiralty | Conrad Hotel | Pacific Pl., 88 Queensway (Queen's Rd. Central) | (852) 2521-3838 | www.conradhotels.com

The service is "top-notch" at this Admiralty "institution" housed in the Conrad Hotel where "reliable" Northern Italian cuisine and an "extensive" wine list are a "nice change from daily dim sum", although some critics find the "expensive" fare "uninspiring"; a collection of "Murano glass" graces the entrance of the eighth-floor space and the view from the windows is "pleasant", but some feel the "setting could be better."

Z NEW Nobu *Japanese*   25 | 24 | 23 | $655

Tsim Sha Tsui | Intercontinental | 18 Salisbury Rd. (Ave. of Stars) | (852) 2721-1211 | www.hongkong-ic.intercontinental.com

A "solid" addition to Nobu Matsuhisa's global "empire", this Tsim Sha Tsui outpost offers "outstanding" "nontraditional" Japanese, including a chef's menu that "always has something special" and "fresh", "super" sushi; a "stellar" harbor view is the backdrop to the Rockwell Group-designed space, which features an undulating ceiling and bamboo-embedded terrazzo walls, while the service is "quick and efficient."

One Harbour Road *Chinese*   25 | 24 | 26 | $557

Wan Chai | Grand Hyatt | 1 Harbour Rd. (Convention Ave.) | (852) 2588-1234 | www.hongkong.grand.hyatt.com

"Impeccable" service, "high-quality" Cantonese fare (including "excellent" dim sum) and a "wonderful" space with a "spectacular view of the harbor" win raves for this Chinese in the Grand Hyatt in Wan Chai; it's "expensive", but that's "the price you pay" for "one of the best fine-dining places on Hong Kong Island."

One-Thirtyone M *French*   – | – | – | VE

Sai Kung | 131 Tseng Tau Village | (852) 2791-2684 | www.one-thirtyone.com

Not many know about this "hidden gem" in Sai Kung, set in a small "re-modeled village house" with the "South China Sea at its doorstep", far "away from the hustle and bustle of the city", where chef Gary Cheuk "pleases your palate" with his "faultless" French cuisine, which is served by an "attentive" staff; cognoscenti commend it as the "perfect spot for a long weekend lunch or romantic dinner"; N.B. prix fixe only.

Opia ●☑ *Australian*   22 | 24 | 20 | $628

Causeway Bay | Jia Hotel | 1 Irving St. (Pennington St.) | (852) 3196-9100 | www.jiahongkong.com

The "opulent decor sets the mood" at this "stylish, sexy" Australian housed in a Philippe Starck–designed boutique hotel in Causeway Bay, where a "who's who of the city" can be seen partaking of chef Dane Clouston's "innovative", Asian-accented Down Under cuisine; while the staff is "friendly", critics feel the service "must improve", especially since it may take a "second mortgage" for some to dine here.

Peak Bar *Continental*   17 | 20 | 16 | $290

Soho | 9-13 Shelley St. (Staunton St.) | (852) 2140-6877 | www.cafedecogroup.com

"Relaxed but oddly classy", this Soho bistro and bar is "one of the nicer places to chill" over "après-work" drinks or "Sunday brunch" for "expats", offering "spectacular views" and "nice people-watching" along what's purportedly the world's longest outdoor escalator; the Continental fare is "reliable", if "nothing to write home about", and while service can be "spotty", the staff is "friendly", at least.

Peak Lookout, The *Continental/Eclectic*   17 | 22 | 16 | $320

The Peak | 121 Peak Rd. | (852) 2849-1000 | www.peaklookout.com.hk

You "can't beat" the "marvelous" view of the sea from one of the island's "best patios" at this "family-friendly" (and "tourist-packed") Continental-Eclectic on the Peak, while the "wonderfully updated" interior of the "beautiful" "rustic" cottage it occupies also has its charms; though the food is "nothing special" and the service merely "passable", the "world-class" vistas make it a "must for the first-time visitor."

NEW Pearl on the Peak *Eclectic*   19 | 20 | 18 | $529

The Peak | The Peak Tower | 128 Peak Rd. | (852) 2849-5123

A "view to die for" from the Peak Tower is the highlight at this "pricey" spin-off of a popular Melbourne restaurant serving "innovative" Eclectic dishes such as the "inspired" signature pearl meat offering in a "minimalist" setting; critics find the fare "ill-focused" and "trying on the taste buds", but with such "spectacular" vistas from the floor-to-ceiling windows, some posit, "who cares what you eat?"

Peking Garden *Chinese*

21 | 16 | 19 | $276

Central | Alexandra House | 16-20 Chater Rd., B1 (Connaught Rd.) | (852) 2526-6456
Taikoo | Cityplaza II | 18 Taikoo Shing Rd., 2nd fl. (Tai Fung Ave.) | (852) 2884-4131
Tsim Sha Tsui | Star House | 3 Salisbury Rd., 3rd fl. (Canton Rd.) | (852) 2735-8211

Though it's "definitely a tourist destination", this "dependable" chain is a "better-than-average" option for "classic" Chinese dishes at "reasonable" prices, including "must-try" Peking duck and "fantastic" beggar's chicken you must order 24 hours in advance; "make reservations" or be "prepared to wait", because they're usually "crowded", but the "noise and bustle are part of the charm."

Petit Pomerol ● *French*

- | - | - | VE

Causeway Bay | 5 Shelter St. (Victoria Park) | (852) 2915-7282

A find for Francophiles hidden on a side street in Causeway Bay, this upscale traditional French spot serves up staples such as coq au vin paired with an "expansive" Gallic-centric wine list befitting a place named after a Bordeaux appellation; the spare, old-world space has a cozy, intimate atmosphere, and "attentive" service is another plus.

ⓩ Petrus *French*

27 | 26 | 27 | $861

Admiralty | Island Shangri-La | Pacific Pl., 56th fl. (Supreme Court Rd.) | (852) 2820-8590 | www.shangri-la.com/island

"Expensive, but worth it" according to *amis,* this haute French in the Island Shangri-La in Admiralty showcases "top-notch" toque Frederic Chabbert's "excellent", "inventive" cuisine, paired with an "amazing" wine selection; the "helpful staff" provides "impeccable" service while "jaw-dropping views" of Victoria Harbour complement the chandelier-lit room that some find "romantic", others a bit "gaudy"; while the tabs might approach the "Chinese GDP", most agree it's the "right place" to "impress a date or client."

NEW Press Room *Continental*

20 | 20 | 16 | $348

Sheung Wan | 108 Hollywood Rd. (Aberdeen St.) | (852) 2525-3444 | www.thepressroom.com.hk

"Hong Kong's answer to Balthazar" is what some call this "buzzy brasserie" in Sheung Wan with a "NY feel" serving a "fantastic, back-to-basics menu" of "no-fuss" Continental fare and a "classy" wine list in a "cool", "roomy" space with plenty of "people-watching" opportunities; what strikes some as "edgy and raw" service, however, is merely "sloppy and inefficient" to others.

Quarterdeck Club *Australian* | 15 | 17 | 18 | $282 |

Tsim Sha Tsui | Harbour City | G53 Ocean Terminal (Canton Rd.) | (852) 2735-8881 ◑

Wan Chai | Fleet Arcade | 1 Lung King St. (Fenwick Pier) | (852) 2827-8882

"When you need your fix" of "bargain Western chow", this Aussie duo is a "reliable" option, offering "nice menu choices" and "eager" service, although foes find the food "forgettable" compared to the "great" waterfront locations; pessimists fear the Wan Chai branch is "fast losing its draw" as an "alfresco dining" option due to nearby "construction and reclamation", and wonder "how long will it have a harbor view."

RED *Californian* | 15 | 17 | 13 | $313 |

Central | IFC Mall | 8 Finance St., 4th fl. (Connaught Rd.) | (852) 8129-8882 | www.pure-red.com

The outside deck with a "stunning view of Victoria Harbour" is a "perfect place for after-work drinks" at this Californian in Central's IFC mall, but "be prepared for self-service", since it "doesn't have a license to serve (liquor) outdoors"; affiliated with the gym Pure Fitness, it offers an all-day menu of "health food", which some find "bland" and "overpriced", but it remains "popular with the 'it' crowd" nonetheless, thanks to its "fantastic" location; N.B. DJs mix Thursday–Saturday nights.

Rice Paper *Vietnamese* | 18 | 18 | 18 | $234 |

Tsim Sha Tsui | Harbour City | Gateway Arcade, Shop 3319, 3rd fl. (Canton Rd.) | (852) 3151-7801

A "nice place" to "meet friends" and "get away from the crowds" in Tsim Sha Tsui, this Vietnamese in the Gateway Arcade offers "good food" and a "casual" vibe in a "cool", contemporary space; the service is "courteous", if "a little slow", and some purists feel the fare may be "trying too hard to be Chinese."

Ruth's Chris Steak House *Steak* | 21 | 18 | 21 | $538 |

Tsim Sha Tsui | Empire Ctr. | 68 Mody Rd. (Mody Ln.) | (852) 2366-6000 | www.ruthschris.com

A "remarkable re-creation so very far from home", this Tsim Sha Tsui link in the "traditional steakhouse" chain provides those "yearning" for a cowboy rib-eye with "excellent", "high-priced" cuts that are especially welcome "now that American beef is back" in the city; most agree that both the food and service are "reliable", though the "dark", masculine environs aren't for everyone, and some sniff "don't waste your time in Hong Kong at a U.S. chain"; N.B. jacket suggested.

Scirocco *Mediterranean*   ∇ 23 | 23 | 17 | $325

Soho | 10-12 Staunton St. (Shelley St.) | (852) 2973-6611 | www.stauntonsgroup.com

It's a "pleasant surprise if you want to eat a light meal" say fans of this Soho Mediterranean perched above the wine bar Staunton's; the menu features small plates from Italy, Spain and the Middle East as well as entrees of tagines, kebabs and paella, plus the "outdoor terrace is a hot commodity", providing a "great view" at lunch, dinner and "happy hour."

NEW 798 Unit & Co *Continental*   ∇ 16 | 15 | 12 | $183

Causeway Bay | Times Sq. | 1 Matheson St., 13th fl. (Russell St.) | (852) 2506-0611

Yes, you're eating "inside a shopping mall", but this Causeway Bay gastropub hints at "NYC" with its airy, loftlike setup featuring floor-to-ceiling windows and a kitchen visible from the dining area; as for the fish 'n' chips and other affordable, modern Continental offerings, most deem them "good", but unremarkable.

Shake 'Em Buns ⊘ *Burgers*   17 | 10 | 11 | $112

Star Street | 2D Star St. (Wing Fung St.) | (852) 2866-2060 | www.shakembuns.com

They "sure know how to grill a burger" say fans about this "tiny joint" on Star Street, where there's "just some counter space" to enjoy a "quick bite" of greasy grub, plus some veggie options too; while it's "one of the few choices" available for such down-home American eats, patrons say it's leading a "new wave" of patty places in town.

Song Cuisine d'Indochine ⊠ *Vietnamese*   ∇ 22 | 16 | 19 | $294

Soho | 75 Hollywood Rd. (Elgin St.) | (852) 2559-0997

Since it's "a little out of the way and hard to find", this "intimate" Vietnamese earns kudos as the "best-kept secret on Hollywood Road", serving "upscale" fare like caramelized spicy prawns and litchi crème brûlée for a "good value"; while it's "tiny" and plainly furnished, the "relaxed", candlelit space provides a "peaceful" retreat from hectic Soho.

Spice Market *Pan-Asian* | 19 | 19 | 18 | $253 |

Tsim Sha Tsui | Marco Polo Prince Hotel | 23 Canton Rd. (Salisbury Rd.) | (852) 2113-6046 | www.marcopolohotels.com

Guests find a "great range" of Pan-Asian food, including sushi, Chinese noodles and Indian curries, at this Tsim Sha Tsui buffet restaurant inside the Marco Polo Prince Hotel; opinions of the quality range from "high" to "adequate", and while some commend the "nice atmosphere", others advise that "many local places are better."

⊠ Spoon by Alain Ducasse *French* | 23 | 25 | 25 | $844 |

Tsim Sha Tsui | Intercontinental | 18 Salisbury Rd. (Ave. of Stars) | (852) 2313-2256 | www.hongkong-ic.intercontinental.com

"Superb" food, "impeccable" service and a "breathtaking view of the harbor" make this "chic" French export in Tsim Sha Tsui's Intercontinental hotel "a must for the total experience"; although some call the "eclectic" menu a bit "odd" (with "small portions"), and wish that star chef "Alain would visit more often", most appreciate the "attention to detail and quality", recommending it for "impressing clients" on your "expense account", or for a "very special date"; P.S. "take a seat before 8 PM to enjoy the light show on the harbor."

Spring Moon *Chinese* | 26 | 25 | 27 | $512 |

Tsim Sha Tsui | The Peninsula | Salisbury Rd. (Nathan Rd.) | (852) 2315-3160 | www.hongkong.peninsula.com

"Sublime" is the word on this "traditional" Cantonese in Tsim Sha Tsui that diners say "sets the standard for Chinese cuisine" across the country, with favorites including "fabulous dim sum" and "heavenly" Peking duck; its "exceptional Peninsula service", "classic art deco design" and "fine tea menu" further elevate the experience, making it well worth the "expensive" tab; N.B. jacket suggested.

Steak House *Steak* | 25 | 24 | 26 | $794 |

Tsim Sha Tsui | Intercontinental | 18 Salisbury Rd. (Ave. of Stars) | (852) 2313-2405 | www.hongkong-ic.intercontinental.com

Carnivores tout this "expense-account" hotel chophouse in Tsim Sha Tsui the "coolest yet hottest steakhouse in Hong Kong", which offers patrons "multiple choices" of steak knives, mustards and salts to complement the "unbelievable" cuts of meats from the Americas, Australia and Japan (including "Kobe beef to die for") and "fabulous salad bar"; oenophiles "love" the wine bar serving some 270 labels, and "proper" service enhances the "warm" ambiance in the otherwise "masculine" setting.

Stoep, The M *African*

▽ 19 | 15 | 15 | $106

Cheung Sha | 32 Lower Cheung Sha Village (Lantau Island south side) | (852) 2980-2699

"Anything but mainstream", this spot "by the sea" in Lower Cheung Sha serves "true" South African cuisine that "isn't expensive"; the decor of the humble tropical shack "isn't great", but the "nice" beach setting makes it a "great spot for lunch after a morning on a junk" or "after a hike."

Stonegrill *Steak*

▽ 18 | 15 | 15 | $432

Soho | 28 Elgin St. (bet. Peel & Shelley Sts.) | (852) 2504-3333 ☽
Tsim Sha Tsui | Harbour City | G319 Ocean Terminal (Canton Rd.) | (852) 2119-0666
www.thestonegrill.com.hk

"Cook it on your own stone!" exclaim enthusiasts about this upscale Soho steakhouse (and its Tsim Sha Tsui sibling) where guests sear their own meat and seafood on a hot rock that's brought to the table; though some call it "kind of cheesy", noting a "good concept but average execution", others think the plush decor and engaging dining experience "work well", especially for a date.

Super Star Seafood *Chinese/Seafood*

20 | 13 | 15 | $265

Tseun Wan | 388 Castle Peak Rd. (Castle Peak Bay) | (852) 2628-0318 | www.superstarrest.com.hk

"Famous for Chinese seafood" and "delicious dim sum", this "local favorite" in Tseun Wan delivers "fresh, fresh, fresh" fish straight from the indoor tanks; since large parties and families like to gather at the banquet tables, it's a festive place (if a bit "noisy" at times) to share a "tasty" feast for a "good value."

☲ Sushi Hiro *Japanese*

28 | 18 | 21 | $531

Causeway Bay | Henry House | 40-42 Yun Ping Rd., 10th fl. (Pak Sha Rd.) | (852) 2882-8752

It's "definitely one of the best sushi restaurants in town" declare diners about this find inside a Causeway Bay office building, serving "ultrafresh fish" that keeps it "popular among a Japanese clientele"; the minimally decorated room is relaxed but formal enough for a business meal, and most agree the "expensive" tab is "reasonable" considering the "excellent" quality – plus "lunch is a great deal"; P.S. be sure to "book ahead."

Thai Basil *Thai* `20` `15` `16` `$203`
Admiralty | Pacific Pl. | 88 Queensway, lower ground fl. (Queen's Rd. Central) | (852) 2537-4682

"Trendy Thai fusion food" with "creative ingredients" attracts customers to this affordable Admiralty "staple" serving "delicious, reliable" dishes and desserts – making it a real "surprise", given its location inside a "major mall"; while the service needs "upgrading", its neon-lit, nightclubby look makes it a popular starter joint for a night on the town.

Tiffin Lounge ● *Continental/Dessert* `23` `22` `23` `$314`
Wan Chai | Grand Hyatt | 1 Harbour Rd. (Convention Ave.) | (852) 2588-1234 | www.hongkong.grand.hyatt.com

Sweet-toothed surveyors are in "heaven" at the Grand Hyatt's Continental/dessert lounge, thanks to the "amazing dessert buffet" with a "range and quality" that are "something to behold", making it a "fantastic way to end an evening", with the strains of live jazz in the background; two large marble staircases connect the stylish space to the grand, 1930s-style hotel lobby one level below.

Tott's Asian Grill & Bar *Continental* `-` `-` `-` `VE`
Causeway Bay | The Excelsior | 281 Gloucester Rd., 34th fl. (Paterson St.) | (852) 2837-6786 | www.excelsiorhongkong.com

The name is an acronym for 'talk of the town' at this luxe Continental in the Excelsior hotel in Causeway Bay, where the windows offer "one of the best views of the harbor", and the recently renovated space boasts silver-blue fabric wall panels, chocolate-toned armchairs and sofas and a stained-glass column above the bar; although some find the fare merely "adequate", live music and "great drink specials" make it a "fun place for a gathering with friends."

Tribute ⊠ *Californian* ▽ `22` `16` `20` `$459`
Soho | 13 Elgin St. (bet. Hollywood Rd. & Staunton St.) | (852) 2135-6645 | www.tribute.com.hk

A "private kitchen that went legit", this "intimate" Soho "oasis" inside a nondescript, windowless exterior offers a "great-value" prix fixe–

FOOD   DECOR   SERVICE   COST

only menu of "unpretentious, inventive" Californian cuisine made with the "freshest" "seasonal ingredients"; fans appreciate the "close attention" the staff pays to diners, and while some find the space "a bit tight", the decor is nonetheless "tasteful."

Tsui Hang Village *Chinese*   21 | 11 | 16 | $297

Central | New World Tower | 16-18 Queen's Rd. Central, 2nd fl. (Ice House St.) | (852) 2524-2012
Sai Kung | Club Marina Cove | 380 Hiram's Hwy. | (852) 2719-4768
Tsim Sha Tsui | Miramar Shopping Ctr. | 132-134 Nathan Rd. (Kimberly Rd.) | (852) 2376-2882

The "no-nonsense" "homestyle" fare is "well presented" at this Cantonese chain that also offers a separate menu of Chinese-American standards such as kung pao shrimp and fortune cookies; "spotty" service and digs "in need of a renovation" may also remind expats of the Chinatowns back home.

Tuk Tuk Thai 🖾🖗 *Thai*   - | - | - | M

Soho | 30 Graham St. (Hollywood Rd.) | (852) 2542-2760

Named after the three-wheeled taxi common in Southeast Asian cities, this "real-deal" Soho Thai transports you to "the streets of Bangkok" with "authentic", moderately priced cuisine and "friendly" service; the decor embodies "simple" (think wood paneling and lamps from Ikea), but that doesn't detract from the "great value."

Verandah, The Ⓜ *Continental*   21 | 25 | 23 | $473

Repulse Bay | Repulse Bay Hotel | 109 Repulse Bay Rd. | (852) 2812-2722 | www.therepulsebay.com

"Re-live the colonial era" at this "elegant", "romantic" Continental housed in "the remains of the historic Repulse Bay Hotel", with a "beautiful view" of the water and a "clubby", "1930s" interior that reminds you of *Love Is a Many-Splendored Thing* (parts of which are set in the hotel); "popular" for its "beautiful, bountiful" Sunday brunch, it's also "the place for high tea", but critics find the "pricey" dinner fare only "so-so."

Victoria City Seafood *Seafood*   23 | 13 | 15 | $337

Wan Chai | Sun Hung Kai Ctr. | 30 Harbour Rd., 2nd fl. (Harbour Dr.) | (852) 2827-9938 | www.eastocean.com.hk

Freshly killed steamed fish is a "standout" at this Wan Chai maritimer that comes "highly recommended", as long as your "budget is not an issue"; service can "depend on whether one is a regular", and the scene in the banquet-style room can get "hectic" and "noisy", but many agree it's an "excellent" venue for "business gatherings and celebrations."

NEW Wagyu *Australian* 22 | 19 | 20 | $504

Central | The Centrium | 60 Wyndham St. (D'Aguilar St.) | (852) 2525-8805

"See and be seen" at this "awesome addition" to the "burgeoning scene on Wyndam Street" in Central where the Australian cuisine featuring the eponymous Japanese-style beef is "consistent and reasonably priced"; the "friendly" service "never disappoints", and though it does get "noisy", the "relaxed", "hip" setting has a "great buzz", especially during the "warm season" when the place becomes "open air."

Wang Fu *Chinese* ∇ 21 | 4 | 10 | $77

Central | Jade Ctr. | 98A Wellington St. (Cochrane St.) | (852) 2121-8006

Thanks to "excellent" Beijing dumplings that are among the "best in town" and über-"reasonable" tabs, you can count on long lines at this bargain Chinese in Central, but "don't expect a cozy environment", for the "very simple" setting "matches the prices"; still, for many it's "perfect for a quick lunch or afternoon snack"; N.B. no alcohol served.

Wasabisabi *Japanese* 19 | 23 | 18 | $444

Causeway Bay | Times Sq. | 1 Matheson St., 13th fl. (Russell St.) | (852) 2506-0009 | www.aqua.com.hk

Enter through a glowing red glass facade and walk a glass colonnade into a "gorgeous", "over-the-top" "modern" space at this "trendy" Causeway Bay Japanese where a section morphs into a nightclub complete with DJ at night; the "well-presented" *washoku* "with a fusion touch" includes "wonderfully creative" sushi, while the service is "attentive" "without being too overbearing"; it's "pricey", but the lunch prix fixe is a "good value."

Water Margin *Chinese* 20 | 23 | 18 | $378

Causeway Bay | Times Sq. | 1 Matheson St., 12th fl. (Russell St.) | (852) 3102-0088 | www.aqua.com.hk

Despite its "odd location in a mega mall" in Causeway Bay, this "hip" Chinese is a popular "place to impress *gweilo*" with its "beautiful" "modern take on classical decor" that reminds some of "old Shanghai" and dimly lit space, where live jazz and traditional puppet shows add to the experience; the "spicy" northern cuisine is "well presented", but critics find the cooking merely "so-so" and feel the "staff could be more helpful."

Xi Yan *Chinese* | 21 | 17 | 15 | $300

Wan Chai | 231-233 E. Queen's Rd., 3rd fl. (Yen Wah Steps Rd. E.) | (852) 9029-9196 | www.xiyan.com.hk

The "consistent quality" of the "innovative" Sichuan cuisine at this Wan Chai private kitchen is "never disappointing" according to fans who lament that it's gotten "hard to book" a table in the stylish, modern dining room; while some grumble that the "menu hasn't changed in years" and is in danger of "becoming mundane", it remains "highly recommended" by those in-the-know.

☑ Yan Toh Heen *Chinese* | 26 | 26 | 28 | $650

Tsim Sha Tsui | Intercontinental | 18 Salisbury Rd. (Ave. of Stars) | (852) 2721-1211 | www.hongkong-ic.intercontinental.com

"Magnificent in every way", this Chinese in Tsim Sha Tsui's Intercontinental hotel is "true decadence", offering "top-notch" service, "splendid" Cantonese cuisine, including some of the "best dim sum in the world", and an "elegant, beautiful" space featuring "jade place settings" and "amazing" views of the harbor; not surprisingly, "you'll pay through the nose", but "oh, is it worth it."

Yee Tung Heen *Chinese* | - | - | - | E

Causeway Bay | The Excelsior | 281 Gloucester Rd. (Paterson St.) | (852) 2837-6790 | www.excelsiorhongkong.com

"Go with a group of foodies" or "VIPs" to this veteran Cantonese in Causeway Bay's Excelsior hotel where the dim sum is "lovely" and the "consistent high-quality" of the entire menu makes it "worth a try"; paintings and ceramics grace the stylish yet simple space with a contemporary Chinese look.

Yellow Door Kitchen *Chinese* | 19 | 12 | 18 | $329

Soho | 37 Cochrane St., 6th fl. (Lynhurst Terrace) | (852) 2858-6555 | www.yellowdoorkitchen.com.hk

One of the original private kitchens that emerged after the financial crisis of the late 1990s, this "hidden gem" in Soho is "unbelievably hard to find", but those who can are rewarded with a "good-value" tasting menu of Sichuan and Shanghainese cooking, including a "divine" eight-treasure duck; "friendly" service and a "relaxed" ambiance help make up for the "uninspired" digs.

Yè Shanghai *Chinese*   23 | 22 | 22 | $420

Admiralty | Pacific Pl. | 88 Queensway, 3rd fl. (Queen's Rd. Central) | (852) 2376-3322
NEW Tsim Sha Tsui | Marco Polo Hotel | 3 Canton Rd. (Salisbury Rd.) | (852) 2376-3322
www.elite-concepts.com

"Xiao long bao to die for" and many other "outstanding" "classic" Shanghainese dishes "with a twist", served in "stylish", "unpretentious" digs with "comfortable" ambiance, make it "worth going" to this "upmarket" duo in Admiralty and Tsim Sha Tsui; family-style portions and tables are well suited to large groups; N.B. jacket suggested.

Yun Fu *Chinese*   ▽ 19 | 21 | 20 | $565

Central | 43-55 Wyndham St. (D'Aguilar St.) | (852) 2116-8855 | www.aqua.com.hk

Enter this Central Chinese through heavy wooden doors and descend a staircase lined with statues of Buddha into a "dungeon"-like subterranean space with "sultry" red lighting, a stylish circular bar and historical decor that evokes ancient China; "helpful" service and "innovative" northern regional dishes also make it "worth a visit."

☑ Yung Kee *Chinese*   23 | 14 | 17 | $298

Central | 32-40 Wellington St. (D'Aguilar St.) | (852) 2522-1624 | www.yungkee.com.hk

A "classic Hong Kong establishment", this "famous" Central landmark (circa 1942) is a "must-try for visitors", serving "generous" portions of "wonderful" "traditional" Cantonese cuisine, including "out-of-this-world" roast goose and "perfectly done" preserved eggs, that "packs in the crowds"; the scene gets "hectic" in the "large", "bright" space that can accommodate "families and large groups", but you "don't come here for the ambiance or service."

NEW Zest *Continental*   22 | 16 | 18 | $412

Central | 57 Wyndham St. (Hollywood Rd.) | (852) 2367-8438

Fans "go away happy" from this "trendy" Continental in Central serving an "interesting menu" of "innovative" dishes and desserts

	FOOD	DECOR	SERVICE	COST

that "should not be skipped"; the contemporary space is "elegant", if "small", and some complain that it's "too expensive for such a casual" setting.

NEW Zuma 🗷 *Japanese*   24 | 26 | 20 | $616

Central | The Landmark | 11 Pedder St., 5th fl. (Queen's Rd. Central) | (852) 3657-6388 | www.zumarestaurant.com

The "new Japanese kid on the block" is this "swank, stylish" spot in Central where "young investment bankers" and other "suits" congregate in a "beautiful", "modern" bi-level space boasting marble-topped sushi and teppanyaki counters, an open kitchen, outdoor patio and upstairs lounge; "creative", "Western"-influenced takes on traditional cuisine are "well executed" and "exciting", though critics deem it "overpriced" and some feel the staff can be "overly attentive" at times.

HOTELS

Most Popular Hotels

1. Peninsula
2. Four Seasons
3. InterContinental
4. Mandarin Oriental
5. Grand Hyatt
6. Conrad
7. JW Marriott
8. Sheraton
9. Island Shangri-La
10. Mandarin Oriental Landmark

Top Overall Ratings

Average of Rooms, Service, Dining and Facilities scores. Excludes places with low votes.

28 Peninsula	Mandarin Oriental Landmark
Four Seasons	InterContinental
26 Island Shangri-La	Conrad
25 Mandarin Oriental	24 Grand Hyatt

Top Rooms

29 Four Seasons	Mandarin Oriental Landmark
28 Peninsula	25 InterContinental
26 Island Shangri-La	Mandarin Oriental

Top Service

28 Four Seasons	27 Island Shangri-La
Peninsula	Mandarin Oriental Landmark
Mandarin Oriental	26 Conrad

Top Dining

28 Peninsula	25 Mandarin Oriental
26 Four Seasons	InterContinental
Island Shangri-La	

Top Facilities

27 Four Seasons	Grand Hyatt
Peninsula	InterContinental
25 Mandarin Oriental Landmark	

subscribe to ZAGAT.com

Hotels

Ratings & Symbols

Rooms, Service, Dining and **Facilities** are rated on the Zagat 0 to 30 scale.

Cost reflects the hotel's high-season rate in Hong Kong dollars for a standard double room. It does not reflect seasonal changes.

- 👪 children's programs
- ✗ exceptional restaurant
- ⊕ historic interest
- ✑ kitchens
- 🐾 allow pets
- 👀 views
- Ⓢ notable spa facilities
- 🏊 swimming
- 🎾 tennis

Conrad 👀🏊 | 25 | 26 | 23 | 24 | $2800 |

Admiralty | Pacific Pl., 88 Queensway | (852) 2521-3838 | fax 2521-3888 | 800-445-8667 | www.conradhotels.com | 467 rooms, 46 suites

With a "superb location" minutes from the Hong Kong Convention and Exhibition Centre in Admiralty and "attached to some of the best shopping" in Pacific Place, this "glamorous" outpost draws raves for a "wonderful staff" and "incredible", "exceptionally furnished" rooms, some with "amazing harbor views"; there's a "fabulous" poolside restaurant where you can dine outside among "trees lit up with tiny white lights", plus a full-service business center and state-of-the-art health club.

Cosmo 👀 | - | - | - | - | $1400 |

Wan Chai | 375-377 E. Queen's Rd. | (852) 3552-8388 | fax 3552-8399 | www.cosmohotel.com.hk | 142 rooms, 2 suites

One of the few overnight options in the Wan Chai bar and entertainment district, this boutique hotel is perfect for night owls who don't mind compact accommodations, as its rooms are some of the smallest in the city; still, details like flat-screen TVs and a hip, retro-style design, accented with pastel shades of orange and yellow, lend it cachet to back up the ambitious rates.

	ROOMS	SERVICE	DINING	FACIL.	COST

Disneyland Hotel ♔☉≋ ▽ 23 | 23 | 19 | 23 | $2200

Lantau Island | Hong Kong Disneyland | (852) 3510-6000 | fax 3510-6333 | www.hongkongdisneyland.com | 387 rooms, 13 suites

If you're looking for "the total Disney experience" when visiting the park, this "expensive" option is "definitely up to the standards" expected, especially when it comes to the "wonderful service"; "beautiful" Victorian-style facilities ("similar to the Grand Floridian" in Orlando, FL) include an on-site spa, rooms with flat-panel TVs and family-friendly dining that features character appearances, but some say the restaurant "choices are limited" overall.

Eaton ≋ ▽ 17 | 17 | 18 | 19 | $1300

Tsim Sha Tsui | 380 Nathan Rd. | (852) 2782-1818 | fax 2782-5563 | www.eaton-hotel.com | 432 rooms, 29 suites

A heated rooftop pool, 24-hour gym and in-room Xboxes on request are just some of the touches that make this "affordable", recently renovated Tsim Sha Tsui hotel a "find" for both businesspeople and families; its cream-toned rooms are basic but comfortable, while the "nice location" offers a respite just off the main tourist center.

Excelsior, The ♨☉☍ 16 | 17 | 18 | 16 | $2400

Causeway Bay | 281 Gloucester Rd. | (852) 2894-8888 | fax 2895-6459 | www.excelsiorhongkong.com | 864 rooms, 21 suites

"Reasonably priced for the business traveler" this 35-year-old Causeway Bay hotel has a "central location" that makes it easy to "walk wherever you need to go" and partake in "neighborhood shopping" and dining, with choices including seven restaurants and bars on-site; visitors also appreciate the "good attitude" of the staff, and while they say the "worn" quarters could use an "update", many of the rooms boast impressive harbor views.

⊿ Four Seasons ✕♨☉≋ 29 | 28 | 26 | 27 | $4200

Central | 8 Finance St. | (852) 3196-8888 | fax 3196-8899 | www.fourseasons.com | 345 rooms, 54 suites

"Always a favorite", this "modern", "world-class" hotel (Hong Kong's No. 1 for Rooms, Service and Facilities) attached to the exclusive IFC mall provides "an experience you'll never forget" from the "fantastic service" to the "massive spa", "heavenly pool" with "breathtaking views of Victoria Harbour", "sleek rooms" and "impeccable restaurants"; it's all "just what you'd expect" from this "top-notch" chain – too bad it can sometimes be "tough to get rooms."

Grand Hyatt ♨Ⓢ≈〰️🔍 | 24 | 23 | 23 | 25 | $3106 |

Wan Chai | 1 Harbour Rd. | (852) 2588-1234 | fax 2802-0677 | www.hongkong.grand.hyatt.com | 500 rooms, 49 suites

Spring for a harbor view on the club floors for "breathtaking vistas" at this "outstanding" spot that's particularly convenient for meetings at the attached Hong Kong Exhibition Centre; the "modern" interiors include an art deco lobby and "coolly styled rooms" with "amazing duvets", the "excellent dining" encompasses a "scrumptious evening dessert buffet" and a "spectacular" 80,000-sq.-ft spa is only topped by an extremely "attentive staff"; the only downside is the "very early '90s"-looking decor and the "inconvenient location" for leisurites.

Harbour Plaza Metropolis ♨Ⓢ≈ | – | – | – | – | $987 |

Hung Hom | 7 Metropolis Dr. | (852) 3160-6888 | fax 3160-6926 | www.harbour-plaza.com | 700 rooms, 120 suites

Surrounded by high-rises and far away from the center, this hotel is most convenient for travelers en route to and from the Chinese mainland due to its location across the street from the Hung Hom KCR train station; while its well-appointed rooms are less opulent than others in the same price bracket, the staff and service are highly polished.

Holiday Inn Golden Mile ♨≈ | 15 | 17 | 14 | 15 | $2500 |

Tsim Sha Tsui | 50 Nathan Rd. | (852) 2369-3111 | fax 2369-8016 | www.holiday-inn.com | 583 rooms, 9 suites

This "massive" hotel in Tsim Sha Tsui is prized for a location that's "close to the subway hubs", "walking distance to the harbor and ferries" and central for "exploring" the energetic surrounding area; while the "executive rooms are big and well appointed", others are merely "basic", but all in all it ranks as a "solid" choice for budget-conscious business travelers and families; N.B. kids 12 and under eat free.

🆕 Hotel LKF ♨ | – | – | – | – | $2470 |

Central | 33 Wyndham St. | (852) 3518-9688 | fax 3518-9699 | www.hotel-lkf.com.hk | 86 rooms, 9 suites

Located on the outskirts of the Lan Kwai Fong bar and club playground in Central, this boutique hotel offers an intimate refuge from the party

	ROOMS	SERVICE	DINING	FACIL.	COST

scene, with spacious, well-designed rooms and suites furnished with Aeron chairs, 42-inch plasma TVs and more; you can shake it to live music every night in the Cavern bar, take in harbor views over cocktails and Continental fare at Azure, or down vodka shots in the minus-20-degree Celsius 'cold room' at the Russian restaurant Balalaika.

InterContinental ✕ 👫 ⓢ ≋

| 25 | 25 | 25 | 25 | $5384 |

Tsim Sha Tsui | 18 Salisbury Rd. | (852) 2721-1211 | fax 2739-4546 | 800-327-0200 | www.hongkong-ic.intercontinental.com | 404 rooms, 91 suites

Fans feel they've "arrived" when they stay at this "first-rate", ultra-modern chain link on the Kowloon waterfront, where they revel in "the most spectacular views" ("there's nothing like waking up to the sights and sounds" of the waterfront or "relaxing in a glass-sided" pool that "visually spills over into" the water below); foodies find "some of the best restaurants in Hong Kong", including Alain Ducasse's Spoon and a branch of the Japanese eatery Nobu, but some just lounge "at dusk with a drink" while "admiring the city lights."

InterContinental Grand Stanford 👫 ⓢ ≋

| 23 | 23 | 21 | 22 | $1600 |

Tsim Sha Tsui | 70 Mody Rd. | (852) 2721-5161 | fax 2732-2233 | www.hongkong.intercontinental.com | 290 rooms, 24 suites

Fans find this chain link in Kowloon's Tsim Sha Tsui East "absolutely fabulous" with the "best service and rooms", particularly if you book a "harbor view" ("magnificent at night"); other highlights at this "home away from home" include a "beautiful" rooftop pool, a fitness center, a spa and several restaurants.

ⓩ Island Shangri-La ✕ 🖥 👫 ≋

| 26 | 27 | 26 | 24 | $5353 |

Admiralty | Supreme Court Rd. | (852) 2877-3838 | fax 2521-8742 | 866-565-5050 | www.shangri-la.com/island | 531 rooms, 34 suites

"Back to the top after an extensive face-lift", this hotel attached to the Pacific Place shopping and business complex in the heart of Admiralty is a "favorite luxury" for those who appreciate "incredible pampering" by a "doting" staff and "modern" rooms, some with "mesmerizing views" of the harbor; it may be a "wee bit isolated" for some, but it's in a "stunning" location for others who like being "set off from the hustle" and bustle.

Jia 🖉🏍

| | - | - | - | - | $2000 |

Causeway Bay | 1-5 Irving St. | (852) 3196-9000 | fax 3196-9001 |
www.jiahongkong.com | 24 suites, 2 penthouses, 28 studios

Designers Philippe Starck and John Hitchcox are behind the first boutique apartment-style hotel for "hipsters" in Hong Kong – this "trendy"
spot in the Causeway Bay area; "ultramod design" that includes teak
floors, white-curtained walls, eclectic chandeliers and African artifacts,
and accommodations that range from studios to two-bedroom duplex
penthouses with marble kitchens and baths, flat-screen TVs and
home-theater systems "set it apart from the standard" – just be fore-
warned, the "cool" factor means "even taxis don't know where it is."

JW Marriott 🏍⑤🏊

| | 22 | 22 | 18 | 21 | $2500 |

Admiralty | Pacific Pl., 88 Queensway | (852) 2810-8366 | fax 2845-5808 |
800-228-9290 | www.marriott.com | 577 rooms, 25 suites

With a "central" location at Pacific Place in Admiralty, this solid business hotel may "not be the best in Hong Kong" but it's "right in the
middle of everything" and offers "surprisingly warm" service, a club
level "worth the extra cost" and an "excellent" 24-hour health club and
spa; still, it's "nothing special" to folks who find a "large, impersonal"
property with somewhat "small" rooms.

Kowloon Shangri-La 🏋🖉🏍🏊

| | 23 | 24 | 20 | 20 | $2887 |

Tsim Sha Tsui | 64 Mody Rd. | (852) 2721-2111 | fax 2723-8686 |
www.shangri-la.com/kowloon | 670 rooms, 30 suites

A "Kowloon classic" with "outstanding interior design and architec-
ture", including recently expanded facilities and renovated health
club, this hotel lures loyalists who like the "happening lobby bar",
quarters with "fabulous views" overlooking the harbor ("worth the extra money") and "incredible" staff that goes "way, way out of its way";
but others say it's merely a "traditional hotel" with a "just ok" restaurant and rooms that "need to be refreshed."

Langham 🏍🏊

| | 20 | 24 | 19 | 19 | $1950 |

Tsim Sha Tsui | 8 Peking Rd. | (852) 2375-1133 | fax 2375-6611 |
www.langhamhotels.com | 469 rooms, 26 suites

Located in Kowloon's touristy Tsim Sha Tsui area, this "charming" recently renovated property excels when it comes to "friendly, helpful"
service", especially on the executive floor where the staff goes "above

and beyond" expectations; other pluses include "large rooms" that are a "godsend", a swimming pool and a 24-hour fitness center.

Langham Place ⚇⑤≋ | ▽ 24 | 25 | 23 | 25 | $1700

Mongkok | 555 Shanghai St. | (852) 3552-3388 | fax 3522-3322 | www.langhamhotels.com | 615 rooms, 50 suites

Building on the 140-plus-year history of Langham Hotels, this high-tech trendsetter in Mongkok is a "hidden jewel" with rooms boasting all the "gadgets" geeksters love (WiFi, flat-screen TVs, DVD/CD players, IP phone) plus floor-to-ceiling windows and baths with rain-shower features; other "excellent" facilities include the Chuan Spa, offering traditonal Chinese medicine, and four restaurants, including a BBQ spot with service under the stars.

Lan Kwai Fong Hotel | - | - | - | - | $2400

Central | 3 Kau U Fong | (852) 3650-0000 | fax 3650-0088 | www.lankwaifonghotel.com.hk | 157 rooms, 5 suites

Overlooking the "trendy" district of Lan Kwai Fong, this "boutique" hotel in Central offers a "refuge from the insanity" of the area's nightlife, with a 24-hour gym and in-room Chinese massages available to help you recover; the compact rooms blend contemporary design with traditional accents, and there are larger harbor-view suites on the top two floors.

Le Méridien Cyberport ⚇≋ | ▽ 26 | 25 | 23 | 23 | $2700

Cyberport | 100 Cyberport Rd. | (852) 2980-7788 | fax 2980-7888 | www.lemeridien.com | 168 rooms, 2 suites

With a "high-tech feel perfect for its location" in the Cyberport complex (aka 'Digital City') on Hong Kong's south side, this "funky" hotel sports "innovative", ultramod rooms (heavy on glass and chrome) and WiFi that allows guests to take calls, check in and surf the Internet from anywhere within the property; some are bothered by an address far from the city center that "isn't ideal for either business or pleasure", but the "relaxed service", on-site wine bar and knockout view of the Lamma Channel make up for it.

ⓃⒺⓌ Luxe Manor, The | - | - | - | - | $2000

Tsim Sha Tsui | 39 Kimberley Rd. | (852) 3763-8888 | fax 3763-8882 | www.theluxemanor.com | 154 rooms, 5 suites

Kowloon's hottest designer boutique hotel, modeled on a European mansion, sports Salvador Dalí-inspired decor (a gigantic pocket watch painted on the lobby floor, abstract chandeliers, whimsical furnishings), along with cutting-edge technology (rooms have WiFi and mirrors that turn into high-def, flat-panel TVs); other highlights include the Italian eatery Aspasia and an on-site fitness center.

☑ Mandarin Oriental ✕⊕♨☉≋   `25` `28` `25` `24` `$3600`

Central | 5 Connaught Rd. | (852) 2522-0111 | fax 2810-6190 | www.mandarinoriental.com | 434 rooms, 68 suites

"Effortless" service is the hallmark of this "ritzy" and "discreet" veteran with the "right address" in the heart of Central's business district when you're on the corporate dime; the "stunning" rooms with "everything you need" are "even better" after recent renovations, but the "legendary service is as good as always" and the "wonderful air of history", "especially in the bar", remains; P.S. don't miss the "exceptional" dining.

Mandarin Oriental
The Landmark ✕⏚☉≋   `26` `27` `23` `25` `$4300`

Central | 15 Queen's Rd. Central | (852) 2132-0188 | fax 2132-0199 | 800-526-6566 | www.mandarinoriental.com | 101 rooms, 12 suites

With a "hip Central location", this "fabulous" hotel has "huge", high-tech rooms with cutting-edge entertainment systems, 400-thread-count linens and a design so stunning "you'll take pictures so you can renovate when you go home"; other highlights include "personalized" service, a "state-of-the-art" fitness center and spa, and chef Richard Ekkebus' "exceptional" modern European haute cuisine at Amber, with interior designed by Adam Tihany.

Marco Polo ♨≋   `15` `20` `16` `16` `$2550`

Tsim Sha Tsui | Harbour City | (852) 2113-0088 | fax 2113-0011 | www.marcopolohotels.com | 513 rooms, 26 suites

"Location, location, location" is the mantra of this waterfront lodging in the heart of Tsim Sha Tsui, a "shopper's delight" that's "convenient" to "great Silk Road shops" and the "Star Ferry"; a "glorious" view of the harbor and "exceptional" service make up for "subpar" dated rooms.

Miramar ♨≋   `-` `-` `-` `-` `$1100`

Tsim Sha Tsui | 118-130 Nathan Rd. | (852) 2315-5555 | fax 2369-0972 | www.hotelmiramar.hk | 512 rooms, 13 suites

One of Hong Kong's toniest hotels in its heyday, blessed with an "excellent" Tsim Sha Tsui location overlooking Kowloon Park, more recently this establishment has been better known as the place where actor Chow Yun Fat spent his formative years as a bellboy; a major renovation was undertaken in late 2007 to restore it to its former glory.

Nikko 🏨🏊

▽ | 18 | 19 | 16 | 15 | $2400

Tsim Sha Tsui | 72 Mody Rd. | (852) 2739-1111 | fax 2311-3122 | www.hotelnikko.com.hk | 445 rooms, 18 suites

A "terrific location" in Tsim Sha Tsui, minutes away from the Star Ferry and MTR station, is the main draw of this "modern" local outpost of a Japan-based chain that caters to businessmen; facilities include a rooftop pool, shopping arcade and nonsmoking floors, and though the rooms are "small", they include amenities such as LCD televisions and broadband access, and some offer views of Victoria Harbour.

Novotel-Citygate 🏊

- | - | - | - | $1100

Tung Chung | 51 Man Tung Rd. | (852) 3602-8888 | fax 2109-9177 | www.novotel.com | 400 rooms, 40 suites

Frequent fliers find a "nice surprise" at this solid Tung Chung hotel just five minutes from the airport and convenient to Disneyland, where "modern" rooms feature satellite TV and WiFi, and facilities include four executive floors, two restaurants and an indoor pool; bargain-hunters are further pleased by the "good" rates at this comfortable spot.

Park Lane, The 🏨

- | - | - | - | $1500

Causeway Bay | 310 Gloucester Rd. | (852) 2293-8888 | fax 2576-7853 | www.parklane.com.hk | 767 rooms, 36 suites

While this large, veteran hotel establishment located across the street from Victoria Park may look like a "basic business" lodging on the outside, inside it "feels like a boutique hotel" to some, thanks to "friendly" service and "dependable", "standard" rooms that have been recently updated, including more than 300 rooms with views of the park and harbor; the "convenient" Causeway Bay location is another plus.

☑ Peninsula, The 👫✗⊕☕🏨⑤🏊

28 | 28 | 28 | 27 | $3699

Tsim Sha Tsui | Salisbury Rd. | (852) 2920-2888 | fax 2722-4170 | www.hongkong.peninsula.com | 246 rooms, 54 suites

"Still the heavyweight champ" (Hong Kong's Most Popular, Top Overall and No. 1 for Dining), this "ultimate" spot in Tsim Sha Tsui "remains the standard" say regulars who "fall in love" with its stunning colonial facade, "amazingly spacious", high-tech rooms, "second-to-none" service and "fabulous" dining that includes the Philippe Starck-designed Felix restaurant; add in the "fleet of Rolls-Royces", an ESPA spa and all that "old-world charm", and most "never want to leave."

Regal Airport ♨Ⓢ≋ | 16 | 14 | 13 | 16 | $2250 |

Chek Lap Kok | 9 Cheong Tat Rd. | (852) 2286-8888 | fax 2286-8686 | www.regalhotel.com | 162 rooms, 17 cabanas

"Excellent for the business traveler", this "large" lodging servicing Hong Kong International Airport is a "convenient" option for an "overnight stay" or even to "freshen up for a few hours" between connections, with more than 1,000 "stark", "modern" rooms and room service fare "delivered hot"; critics, though, find the facilities merely "functional" and "overpriced", and sniff the "location" is the "only reason to stay here."

Renaissance Harbor View ♨≋✎ | 19 | 21 | 19 | 19 | $3200 |

Wan Chai | 1 Harbour Rd. | Renaissance Harbor | fax 2802-8833 | www.marriott.com | 737 rooms, 123 suites

Appended to the Hong Kong Convention and Exhibition Centre, this newly renovated chain link in Wan Chai offers a "great location" for business with "beautiful" views of the harbor and an "active bar scene"; though a few find that the rooms "leave something to be desired compared to the competition" (something a recent renovation may help remedy), service that's "much better than expected" makes it a "solid" choice.

Renaissance Kowloon ≋ | - | - | - | - | $1080 |

Tsim Sha Tsui | 22 Salisbury Rd. | (852) 2369-4111 | fax 2369-9387 | www.marriott.com | 439 rooms, 53 suites

One of Hong Kong's oldest hotels, this chain link in the heart of Tsim Sha Tsui offers easy access to the area's business, cultural and shopping scenes, as well as bus, ferry or train transportation; it also boasts an outdoor pool as well as a fitness center, and dining options include Cantonese fare and dim sum at the Dynasty restaurant and stunning harbor views and Continental cuisine at the aptly named Panorama.

Royal Garden, The ♨≋ | - | - | - | - | $2900 |

Tsim Sha Tsui | 69 Mody Rd. | (852) 2721-5215 | fax 2311-2985 | www.rghk.com.hk | 374 rooms, 48 suites

All of the 374 rooms and 48 suites at this Tsim Sha Tsui hotel offer terraced balconies overlooking its famous 17-story-high, skylit atrium filled with elegant aqueducts and lush foliage; after playing a few sets of tennis on the court or swimming a few laps in the pool on top of the roof, you can unwind with a drink at the lobby's Martini Bar before a dinner of Japanese fare at Inagiku.

Royal Park Hotel ♨☱♣   - | - | - | - | $1000

Shatin | 8 Pak Hok Ting St. | (852) 2601-2111 | fax 2601-3666 | www.royalpark.com.hk | 431 rooms, 12 suites

"Chain-resistant travelers" and those who prefer the greenery of the New Territories to the glass and steel of the city can find classy lodgings in these twin towers conveniently located in the heart of Shatin, overlooking its verdant park and the Shing Mun River; the elegantly appointed rooms feature marble-tiled bathrooms, satellite TV and broadband access, and the dining options include Chinese, Chiu Chow and Japanese cuisines, as well as an all-day international buffet.

Salisbury YMCA ♨☱   - | - | - | - | $820

Tsim Sha Tsui | 41 Salisbury Rd. | (852) 2268-7000 | fax 2739-9315 | www.ymcahk.org | 301 rooms, 62 suites

What it may lack in cachet, this Tsim Sha Tsui Y more than makes up for with a prime waterfront location offering outstanding views of Victoria Harbour and Hong Kong Island, as well as surprisingly cushy facilities that include an indoor pool, fitness center and hair salon, as well as an Eclectic buffet and a self-service cafe, both open all day; the rooms range from dormitory-style to private to family and business suites, all at bargain rates.

Sheraton Hong Kong Hotel & Towers ✗♨Ⓢ☱   21 | 21 | 20 | 20 | $3100

Tsim Sha Tsui | 20 Nathan Rd. | (852) 2369-1111 | fax 2739-8707 | www.starwoodhotels.com | 754 rooms, 28 suites

Loyalists of this often "crowded" harborside chain link in Tsim Sha Tsui "love the rooftop pool with gorgeous views of Hong Kong", the "heavenly beds" and the "convenient" location with "many sights within walking distance"; but others contend the "good, not great" service and "tired decor" that "lacks the splendor" of its competitors make it a "so-so", "basic" "businessman's" choice.

INDEXES

Dining Cuisines

Includes restaurant names, locations and Food ratings. ☑ indicates places with the highest ratings, popularity and importance.

AMERICAN (NEW)

Harlan's | **Central** | 20

AMERICAN (TRADITIONAL)

Al's Diner | **Lan Kwai Fong** | 17
Craftsteak | **Soho** | 22
Dan Ryan's | **Admiralty** | 16
Shake 'Em Buns | **Star Street** | 17

ASIAN

Cafe Deco | **The Peak** | 18

ASIAN FUSION

Bo Innovation | **Central** | 20

AUSTRALIAN

Opia | **Causeway Bay** | 22
Quarterdeck Club | **multi.** | 15
NEW Wagyu | **Central** | 22

AUSTRIAN

Mozart Stub'n | **Central** | 20

BURGERS

Dan Ryan's | **Admiralty** | 16
Shake 'Em Buns | **Star Street** | 17

CAJUN

Magnolia | **Sheung Wan** | 25

CALIFORNIAN

Bizou Bistro | **Soho** | 18
RED | **Central** | 15
Tribute | **Soho** | 22

CHINESE

(* dim sum specialist)
Bistro Manchu | **Soho** | 18
☑ China Club | **Central** | 22
China Tee | **Central** | 18
Chiu Chow | **Central** | 21
☑ Crystal Jade | **Tsim Sha Tsui** | 23
Cuisine Cuisine | **Central** | 18
Da Ping Huo | **Soho** | 24
Dim Sum* | **Happy Valley** | 25
Dong Lai Shun | **Tsim Sha Tsui** | –
Dragon-I | **Central** | 18
Fai Sea | **Kowloon City** | –
Farm House | **Causeway Bay** | 23
☑ Fook Lam Moon | **Wan Chai** | 26
Green T. House | **Cyberport** | 17
☑ Hutong | **Tsim Sha Tsui** | 24
Jumbo | **Wong Chuk Hang** | 16
Kin's Kitchen | **North Point** | 22
Lei Garden | **multi.** | 24
Luk Yu Tea* | **Central** | 20
Lumiere | **Central** | 18
☑ Lung King Heen | **Central** | 28
Man Wah | **Central** | 26
Maxim's* | **Central** | 22
Modern China | **Causeway Bay** | –
New Dynasty | **Wan Chai** | –
1 Harbour Road | **Wan Chai** | 25
Peking Garden | **multi.** | 21
Spring Moon | **Tsim Sha Tsui** | 26
Super Star | **Tseun Wan** | 20
Tsui Hang Village | **multi.** | 21
Wang Fu | **Central** | 21

Water Margin	**Causeway Bay**	20
Xi Yan	**Wan Chai**	21
Ⓩ Yan Toh Heen	**Tsim Sha Tsui**	26
Yee Tung Heen	**Causeway Bay**	–
Yellow Door	**Soho**	19
Yè Shanghai	**multi.**	23
Yun Fu	**Central**	19
Ⓩ Yung Kee	**Central**	23

CONTINENTAL

Amber	**Central**	22
Avenue	**Tsim Sha Tsui**	–
Azure	**Lan Kwai Fong**	19
Bayside Brasserie	**Stanley**	17
Boathouse	**Stanley**	20
NEW Bricolage 62	**Soho**	18
Cafe Deco	**The Peak**	18
Café Landmark	**Central**	16
China Tee	**Central**	18
Ⓩ Felix	**Tsim Sha Tsui**	21
Gough 40	**Sheung Wan**	–
Grill/Plateau	**Wan Chai**	–
Ingredients	**Star Street**	16
Jaspa's	**Soho**	18
Jimmy's Kitchen	**multi.**	20
Kee Club	**Lan Kwai Fong**	20
Peak Bar	**Soho**	17
Peak Lookout	**The Peak**	17
NEW Press Room	**Sheung Wan**	20
NEW 798 Unit	**Causeway Bay**	16
Tiffin Lounge	**Wan Chai**	23
Tott's	**Causeway Bay**	–
Verandah	**Repulse Bay**	21
NEW Zest	**Central**	22

DESSERT

Tiffin Lounge	**Wan Chai**	23

ECLECTIC

Black Sheep	**Shek O**	21
Bo Innovation	**Central**	20
Café TOO	**Admiralty**	23
Ⓩ Lobby/Peninsula	**Tsim Sha Tsui**	22
Mandarin Grill	**Central**	25
Peak Lookout	**The Peak**	17
NEW Pearl on Peak	**The Peak**	19

EGYPTIAN

Habibi	**Central**	19

ENGLISH

Chinnery, The	**Central**	23
Clipper Lounge	**Central**	22
Dot Cod	**Central**	19
Ⓩ Lobby/Peninsula	**Tsim Sha Tsui**	22

FRENCH

NEW Agnès B.	**Causeway Bay**	15
Amber	**Central**	22
Amigo	**Happy Valley**	22
Black Sheep	**Shek O**	21
Ⓩ Caprice	**Central**	25
Chez Patrick	**multi.**	20
Cococabana	**Deep Water Bay**	16
Ⓩ Gaddi's	**Tsim Sha Tsui**	27
Gough 40	**Sheung Wan**	–
NEW La Mer	**Lan Kwai Fong**	–
Ⓩ NEW L'Atelier/Robuchon	**Central**	27
M/Fringe	**Central**	24
One-Thirtyone	**Sai Kung**	–
Petit Pomerol	**Causeway Bay**	–
Ⓩ Petrus	**Admiralty**	27
Ⓩ Spoon	**Tsim Sha Tsui**	23

GASTROPUB

NEW 798 Unit | Continental | Causeway Bay ... 16

HEALTH FOOD

Life Café | Soho ... 15

INDIAN

Babek | Soho ... -
Bombay Dreams | Central ... 24
Gaylord | Tsim Sha Tsui ... -

INDONESIAN

Dirty Duck | Wan Chai ... -
Indonesian Rest. | Causeway Bay ... 19

IRISH

McSorley's | multi. ... 11

ITALIAN

Amaroni's | Kowloon Tong ... 15
Aqua | Tsim Sha Tsui ... 19
Baci Pizza | Lan Kwai Fong ... 17
Cinecittà | Star Street ... 19
Ciprani's | Central ... 23
Cova | Causeway Bay ... 19
Da Domenico | Causeway Bay ... 26
Di Vino | Central ... 23
Gaia | Sheung Wan ... 25
Grissini | Wan Chai ... 23
Habitu | Causeway Bay ... 14
Isola | Central ... 22
Nicholini's | Admiralty ... 23

JAPANESE

(* sushi specialist)
Aqua | Tsim Sha Tsui ... 19
Dozo! | Soho ... 13
Dragon-I | Central ... 18
Imasa* | Tsim Sha Tsui ... -
Inagiku* | multi. ... 25
Kenjo's* | Tsim Sha Tsui ... 29
Mi-Ne* | Causeway Bay ... 18
Nadaman | Admiralty ... 26
Z NEW Nobu | Tsim Sha Tsui ... 25
Z Sushi Hiro* | Causeway Bay ... 28
Wasabisabi | Causeway Bay ... 19
NEW Zuma | Central ... 24

KOREAN

Kaya Korean | Causeway Bay ... 19

LEBANESE

Beirut | Lan Kwai Fong ... 19

MEDITERRANEAN

Cococabana | Deep Water Bay ... 16
M/Fringe | Central ... 24
Scirocco | Soho ... 23

MEXICAN

Agave | Lan Kwai Fong ... 10

MONGOLIAN

Dong Lai Shun | Tsim Sha Tsui ... -
Little Sheep | multi. ... 22

PAN-ASIAN

Chilli N Spice | multi. ... 19
Spice Market | Tsim Sha Tsui ... 19

RUSSIAN

Balalaika | Lan Kwai Fong ... 16

SCANDINAVIAN

FINDS | Lan Kwai Fong ... 17

SEAFOOD

Dot Cod | Central ... 19
Fish Bar | Admiralty ... 20
Frog Faced Fish | Central ... 16

Jumbo | **Wong Chuk Hang** 16

NEW La Mer | **Lan Kwai Fong** -

Super Star | **Tseun Wan** 20

Victoria City | **Wan Chai** 23

SOUTH AFRICAN

Stoep, The | **Cheung Sha** 19

SOUTHERN

Magnolia | **Sheung Wan** 25

SPANISH

(* tapas specialist)

Boca Tapas* | **Soho** 20

STEAKHOUSES

Craftsteak | **Soho** 22

Dan Ryan's | **Admiralty** 16

Harlan's | **Central** 20

Morton's | **Tsim Sha Tsui** 26

Ruth's Chris | **Tsim Sha Tsui** 21

Steak House | **Tsim Sha Tsui** 25

Stonegrill | **multi.** 18

THAI

NEW Lian | **Central** 20

Thai Basil | **Admiralty** 20

Tuk Tuk Thai | **Soho** -

VIETNAMESE

Indochine 1929 | **Lan Kwai Fong** 22

NEW Lian | **Central** 20

Nha Trang | **Central** 22

Rice Paper | **Tsim Sha Tsui** 18

Song Cuisine | **Soho** 22

DINING

CUISINES

Dining Locations

Includes restaurant names, cuisines and Food ratings. **Z** indicates places with the highest ratings, popularity and importance.

ADMIRALTY

Café TOO	*Eclectic*	23
Dan Ryan's	*Amer.*	16
Fish Bar	*Seafood*	20
Nadaman	*Japanese*	26
Nicholini's	*Italian*	23
Z Petrus	*French*	27
Thai Basil	*Thai*	20
Yè Shanghai	*Chinese*	23

CAUSEWAY BAY

NEW Agnès B.	*French*	15
Cova	*Italian*	19
Da Domenico	*Italian*	26
Farm House	*Chinese*	23
Habitu	*Italian*	14
Indonesian Rest.	*Indonesian*	19
Kaya Korean	*Korean*	19
Little Sheep	*Mongolian*	22
Mi-Ne	*Japanese*	18
Modern China	*Chinese*	-
Opia	*Australian*	22
Petit Pomerol	*French*	-
NEW 798 Unit	*Continental*	16
Z Sushi Hiro	*Japanese*	28
Tott's	*Continental*	-
Wasabisabi	*Japanese*	19
Water Margin	*Chinese*	20
Yee Tung Heen	*Chinese*	-

CENTRAL

Amber	*Continental/French*	22
Bo Innovation	*Asian Fusion/Eclectic*	20
Bombay Dreams	*Indian*	24
Café Landmark	*Continental*	16
Z Caprice	*French*	25
Z China Club	*Chinese*	22
China Tee	*Chinese/Continental*	18
Chinnery, The	*English*	23
Chiu Chow	*Chinese*	21
Ciprani's	*Italian*	23
Clipper Lounge	*English*	22
Cuisine Cuisine	*Chinese*	18
Di Vino	*Italian*	23
Dot Cod	*English/Seafood*	19
Dragon-I	*Chinese/Japanese*	18
Frog Faced Fish	*Seafood*	16
Habibi	*African*	19
Harlan's	*Amer.*	20
Inagiku	*Japanese*	25
Isola	*Italian*	22
Jimmy's Kitchen	*Continental*	20
Z NEW L'Atelier/Robuchon	*French*	27
Lei Garden	*Chinese*	24
NEW Lian	*Thai/Viet.*	20
Luk Yu Tea	*Chinese*	20
Lumiere	*Chinese*	18
Z Lung King Heen	*Chinese*	28
Mandarin Grill	*Eclectic*	25
Man Wah	*Chinese*	26
M/Fringe	*French/Med.*	24
Maxim's	*Chinese*	22
Mozart Stub'n	*Austrian*	20
Nha Trang	*Viet.*	22
Peking Garden	*Chinese*	21

RED | *Calif.* 15

Tsui Hang Village | *Chinese* 21

NEW Wagyu | *Australian* 22

Wang Fu | *Chinese* 21

Yun Fu | *Chinese* 19

Z Yung Kee | *Chinese* 23

NEW Zest | *Continental* 22

NEW Zuma | *Japanese* 24

CHEUNG SHA

Stoep, The | *African* 19

CYBERPORT

Green T. House | *Chinese* 17

DEEP WATER BAY

Cococabana | *French/Med.* 16

HAPPY VALLEY

Amigo | *French* 22

Dim Sum | *Chinese* 25

KOWLOON CITY

Fai Sea | *Chinese* -

Lei Garden | *Chinese* 24

KOWLOON TONG

Amaroni's | *Italian* 15

LAN KWAI FONG

Agave | *Mex.* 10

Al's Diner | *Amer.* 17

Azure | *Continental* 19

Baci Pizza | *Italian* 17

Balalaika | *Russian* 16

Beirut | *Mideast.* 19

FINDS | *Scan.* 17

Indochine 1929 | *Viet.* 22

Kee Club | *Continental* 20

NEW La Mer | *French/Seafood* -

LANTAU ISLAND

McSorley's | *Irish* 11

MONGKOK

Lei Garden | *Chinese* 24

Little Sheep | *Mongolian* 22

NORTH POINT

Kin's Kitchen | *Chinese* 22

Lei Garden | *Chinese* 24

PEAK, THE

Cafe Deco | *Asian/Continental* 18

Peak Lookout |
Continental/Eclectic 17

NEW Pearl on Peak | *Eclectic* 19

REPULSE BAY

Verandah | *Continental* 21

SAI KUNG

One-Thirtyone | *French* -

Tsui Hang Village | *Chinese* 21

SAI WAN

Chilli N Spice | *Pan-Asian* 19

SHEK O

Black Sheep | *Eclectic/French* 21

SHEUNG WAN

Gaia | *Italian* 25

Gough 40 | *Continental/French* -

Magnolia | *Cajun/Southern* 25

NEW Press Room | *Continental* 20

SOHO

Babek | *Indian* -

Bistro Manchu | *Chinese* 18

Bizou Bistro | *Calif.* 18

Boca Tapas | *Spanish* 20

NEW Bricolage 62 | *Continental* 18

Chez Patrick | *French* 20

Craftsteak | *Steak* 22

Da Ping Huo | *Chinese* 24

Dozo! | *Japanese* — 13

Jaspa's | *Continental* — 18

Life Café | *Health* — 15

McSorley's | *Irish* — 11

Peak Bar | *Continental* — 17

Scirocco | *Med.* — 23

Song Cuisine | *Viet.* — 22

Stonegrill | *Steak* — 18

Tribute | *Californian* — 22

Tuk Tuk Thai | *Thai* — -

Yellow Door | *Chinese* — 19

STANLEY

Bayside Brasserie | *Continental* — 17

Boathouse | *Continental* — 20

Chilli N Spice | *Pan-Asian* — 19

STAR STREET

Chez Patrick | *French* — 20

Cinecittà | *Italian* — 19

Ingredients | *Continental* — 16

Shake 'Em Buns | *Burgers* — 17

TAIKOO

Peking Garden | *Chinese* — 21

TSEUN WAN

Little Sheep | *Mongolian* — 22

Super Star | *Chinese/Seafood* — 20

TSIM SHA TSUI

Aqua | *Italian/Japanese* — 19

Avenue | *Continental* — -

 Z Crystal Jade | *Chinese* — 23

Dong Lai Shun | *Chinese/Mongolian* — -

Z Felix | *Continental* — 21

Z Gaddi's | *French* — 27

Gaylord | *Indian* — -

Z Hutong | *Chinese* — 24

Imasa | *Japanese* — -

Inagiku | *Japanese* — 25

Jimmy's Kitchen | *Continental* — 20

Kenjo's | *Japanese* — 29

Lei Garden | *Chinese* — 24

Little Sheep | *Mongolian* — 22

Z Lobby/Peninsula | *Eclectic/English* — 22

Morton's | *Steak* — 26

Z NEW Nobu | *Japanese* — 25

Peking Garden | *Chinese* — 21

Quarterdeck Club | *Australian* — 15

Rice Paper | *Viet.* — 18

Ruth's Chris | *Steak* — 21

Spice Market | *Pan-Asian* — 19

Z Spoon | *French* — 23

Spring Moon | *Chinese* — 26

Steak House | *Steak* — 25

Stonegrill | *Steak* — 18

Tsui Hang Village | *Chinese* — 21

Z Yan Toh Heen | *Chinese* — 26

Yè Shanghai | *Chinese* — 23

WAN CHAI

Dirty Duck | *SE Asian* — -

Z Fook Lam Moon | *Chinese* — 26

Grill/Plateau | *Continental* — -

Grissini | *Italian* — 23

Lei Garden | *Chinese* — 24

New Dynasty | *Chinese* — -

1 Harbour Road | *Chinese* — 25

Quarterdeck Club | *Australian* — 15

Tiffin Lounge | *Continental/Dessert* — 23

Victoria City | *Seafood* — 23

Xi Yan | *Chinese* — 21

WONG CHUK HANG

Jumbo | *Chinese/Seafood* — 16

Dining Special Features

Listings cover the best in each category and include names, locations and Food ratings. Multi-location restaurants' features may vary by branch. ☒ indicates places with the highest ratings, popularity and importance.

BREAKFAST

(See also Hotel Dining)

Boathouse	Stanley	20
Café Landmark	Central	16
Cova	Causeway Bay	19
Dim Sum	Happy Valley	25
Dot Cod	Central	19
Jaspa's	Soho	18
☒ NEW L'Atelier/Robuchon	Central	27
Life Café	Soho	15
Luk Yu Tea	Central	20
Maxim's	Central	22
New Dynasty	Wan Chai	-
Peak Bar	Soho	17
Super Star	Tseun Wan	20
NEW Wagyu	Central	22

BRUNCH

Aqua	Tsim Sha Tsui	19
Bayside Brasserie	Stanley	17
Bizou Bistro	Soho	18
Bombay Dreams	Central	24
NEW Bricolage 62	Soho	18
Cafe Deco	The Peak	18
Café Landmark	Central	16
☒ China Club	Central	22
China Tee	Central	18
Ciprani's	Central	23
Frog Faced Fish	Central	16
Habitu	Causeway Bay	14
Isola	Central	22

Jaspa's	Soho	18
Jumbo	Wong Chuk Hang	16
Life Café	Soho	15
Lumiere	Central	18
Mandarin Grill	Central	25
McSorley's	Soho	11
Peak Lookout	The Peak	17
NEW Press Room	Sheung Wan	20
Quarterdeck Club	Wan Chai	15
RED	Central	15
Scirocco	Soho	23
NEW 798 Unit	Causeway Bay	16
Super Star	Tseun Wan	20
Tiffin Lounge	Wan Chai	23
Tott's	Causeway Bay	-
Verandah	Repulse Bay	21
NEW Wagyu	Central	22
NEW Zest	Central	22

BUFFET

(Check availability)

Azure	Lan Kwai Fong	19
Bombay Dreams	Central	24
Café TOO	Admiralty	23
Ciprani's	Central	23
Clipper Lounge	Central	22
Grill/Plateau	Wan Chai	-
Lumiere	Central	18
Spice Market	Tsim Sha Tsui	19
Tiffin Lounge	Wan Chai	23

Tott's | **Causeway Bay** — |
Verandah | **Repulse Bay** 21 |

BUSINESS DINING

Amber | **Central** 22 |
Azure | **Lan Kwai Fong** 19 |
Z Caprice | **Central** 25 |
Ciprani's | **Central** 23 |
Da Domenico | **Causeway Bay** 26 |
Dot Cod | **Central** 19 |
Z Felix | **Tsim Sha Tsui** 21 |
Z Gaddi's | **Tsim Sha Tsui** 27 |
Grill/Plateau | **Wan Chai** — |
Grissini | **Wan Chai** 23 |
Harlan's | **Central** 20 |
Inagiku | **Central** 25 |
Ingredients | **Star Street** 16 |
Isola | **Central** 22 |
Jimmy's Kitchen | **Central** 20 |
Kee Club | **Lan Kwai Fong** 20 |
Z NEW L'Atelier/Robuchon | **Central** 27 |
Lei Garden | **Mongkok** 24 |
Lumiere | **Central** 18 |
Z Lung King Heen | **Central** 28 |
Mandarin Grill | **Central** 25 |
M/Fringe | **Central** 24 |
Nadaman | **Admiralty** 26 |
Z NEW Nobu | **Tsim Sha Tsui** 25 |
1 Harbour Road | **Wan Chai** 25 |
Z Petrus | **Admiralty** 27 |
NEW Press Room | **Sheung Wan** 20 |
Ruth's Chris | **Tsim Sha Tsui** 21 |
Z Spoon | **Tsim Sha Tsui** 23 |
Spring Moon | **Tsim Sha Tsui** 26 |
Yè Shanghai | **multi.** 23 |
NEW Zuma | **Central** 24 |

CELEBRITY CHEFS

Bo Innovation | *Alvin Leung* | **Central** 20 |
Z NEW L'Atelier/Robuchon | *Joël Robuchon* | **Central** 27 |
Z Spoon | *Alain Ducasse* | **Tsim Sha Tsui** 23 |

DANCING

Agave | **Lan Kwai Fong** 10 |
Dragon-I | **Central** 18 |

DESSERT

Cova | **Causeway Bay** 19 |
Z Gaddi's | **Tsim Sha Tsui** 27 |
Tiffin Lounge | **Wan Chai** 23 |

DINING ALONE

(Other than hotels and places with counter service)
NEW Bricolage 62 | **Soho** 18 |
China Tee | **Central** 18 |
Z Crystal Jade | **Tsim Sha Tsui** 23 |
Dozo! | **Soho** 13 |
Habibi | **Central** 19 |
NEW Lian | **Central** 20 |
Life Café | **Soho** 15 |
Mi-Ne | **Causeway Bay** 18 |
Nha Trang | **Central** 22 |
Tuk Tuk Thai | **Soho** — |
Wang Fu | **Central** 21 |

DRAMATIC INTERIORS

Amaroni's | **Kowloon Tong** 15 |
Aqua | **Tsim Sha Tsui** 19 |
Azure | **Lan Kwai Fong** 19 |
Cafe Deco | **The Peak** 18 |
Z Caprice | **Central** 25 |
Z China Club | **Central** 22 |
Cococabana | **Deep Water Bay** 16 |

Cova	**Causeway Bay**	19
Dirty Duck	**Wan Chai**	-
Dragon-I	**Central**	18
⊿ Felix	**Tsim Sha Tsui**	21
Grill/Plateau	**Wan Chai**	-
Habitu	**Causeway Bay**	14
⊿ Hutong	**Tsim Sha Tsui**	24
Ingredients	**Star Street**	16
Isola	**Central**	22
Kee Club	**Lan Kwai Fong**	20
NEW La Mer	**Lan Kwai Fong**	-
⊿ NEW L'Atelier/Robuchon	**Central**	27
⊿ Lobby/Peninsula	**Tsim Sha Tsui**	22
Lumiere	**Central**	18
Man Wah	**Central**	26
New Dynasty	**Wan Chai**	-
Peak Lookout	**The Peak**	17
⊿ Spoon	**Tsim Sha Tsui**	23
Verandah	**Repulse Bay**	21
Wasabisabi	**Causeway Bay**	19
Water Margin	**Causeway Bay**	20
Yun Fu	**Central**	19
NEW Zuma	**Central**	24

ENTERTAINMENT

(Call for days and times of performances)

Amigo	band	**Happy Valley**	22
Azure	DJ	**Lan Kwai Fong**	19
Beirut	DJ	**Lan Kwai Fong**	19
Da Ping Huo	Chinese opera	**Soho**	24
Dragon-I	DJ	**Central**	18
FINDS	DJ	**Lan Kwai Fong**	17
Kee Club	DJ	**Lan Kwai Fong**	20
⊿ Lobby/Peninsula	string orchestra	**Tsim Sha Tsui**	22

Peak Lookout	band	**The Peak**	17
⊿ Petrus	piano	**Admiralty**	27
RED	DJ	**Central**	15
Tiffin Lounge	piano	**Wan Chai**	23
Tott's	cover band	**Causeway Bay**	-
Verandah	piano	**Repulse Bay**	21
Yun Fu	DJ	**Central**	19
NEW Zuma	DJ	**Central**	24

HISTORIC PLACES

(Year opened; * building)

1845	Chilli N Spice*	**Stanley**	19
1920	Gaddi's*	**Tsim Sha Tsui**	27
1920	Verandah	**Repulse Bay**	21
1928	Felix*	**Tsim Sha Tsui**	21
1928	Jimmy's Kitchen	**Central**	20
1928	Lobby/Peninsula*	**Tsim Sha Tsui**	22
1928	Spring Moon	**Tsim Sha Tsui**	26
1942	Yung Kee	**Central**	23

HOTEL DINING

Conrad

Nicholini's	**Admiralty**	23

Excelsior

Tott's	**Causeway Bay**	-
Yee Tung Heen	**Causeway Bay**	-

Four Seasons

⊿ Caprice	**Central**	25
Inagiku	**Central**	25
⊿ Lung King Heen	**Central**	28

Grand Hyatt

Grill/Plateau	**Wan Chai**	-
Grissini	**Wan Chai**	23
1 Harbour Road	**Wan Chai**	25
Tiffin Lounge	**Wan Chai**	23

Holiday Inn Golden Mile
  Avenue | **Tsim Sha Tsui**   ‑⌐

Hotel LKF
  Azure | **Lan Kwai Fong**   19⌐

Intercontinental
  Z NEW Nobu | 25⌐
    Tsim Sha Tsui
  Z Spoon | **Tsim Sha Tsui**   23⌐
  Steak House | **Tsim Sha Tsui**   25⌐
  Z Yan Toh Heen | 26⌐
    Tsim Sha Tsui

Island Shangri-La
  Café TOO | **Admiralty**   23⌐
  Nadaman | **Admiralty**   26⌐
  Z Petrus | **Admiralty**   27⌐

Jia
  Opia | **Causeway Bay**   22⌐

JW Marriott
  Fish Bar | **Admiralty**   20⌐

Mandarin Oriental
  Chinnery, The | **Central**   23⌐
  Clipper Lounge | **Central**   22⌐
  Mandarin Grill | **Central**   25⌐
  Man Wah | **Central**   26⌐

Mandarin Oriental Landmark
  Amber | **Central**   22⌐

Marco Polo
  Yè Shanghai | **Tsim Sha Tsui**   23⌐

Marco Polo Prince
  Spice Market | **Tsim Sha Tsui** 19⌐

Peninsula
  Z Felix | **Tsim Sha Tsui**   21⌐
  Z Gaddi's | **Tsim Sha Tsui** 27⌐
  Imasa | **Tsim Sha Tsui**   ‑⌐
  Z Lobby/Peninsula | 22⌐
    Tsim Sha Tsui
  Spring Moon | **Tsim Sha Tsui**   26⌐

Repulse Bay
  Verandah | **Repulse Bay**   21⌐

Royal Garden
  Dong Lai Shun | **Tsim Sha Tsui** ‑⌐
  Inagiku | **Tsim Sha Tsui**   25⌐

Sheraton
  Morton's | **Tsim Sha Tsui**   26⌐

JACKET REQUIRED

Z China Club | **Central**   22⌐
Z Gaddi's | **Tsim Sha Tsui**   27⌐
Z Petrus | **Admiralty**   27⌐

LATE DINING

(Weekday closing hour)

Agave | 1 AM | **Lan Kwai Fong**   10⌐
Al's Diner | 12 AM | 17⌐
  Lan Kwai Fong
Balalaika | 1:30 AM | 16⌐
  Lan Kwai Fong
Boca Tapas | 1:30 AM | **Soho**   20⌐
Cafe Deco | 12 AM | **The Peak**   18⌐
Z China Club | 1 AM | **Central** 22⌐
Cuisine Cuisine | 12 AM | 18⌐
  Central
Dim Sum | 24 hrs. | **Happy Valley** 25⌐
Fai Sea | 2 AM | **Kowloon City**   ‑⌐
Z Felix | 1:30 AM | 21⌐
  Tsim Sha Tsui
FINDS | 12 AM | **Lan Kwai Fong**   17⌐
Gaia | 12 AM | **Sheung Wan**   25⌐
Gough 40 | 12 AM | ‑⌐
  Sheung Wan
Green T. House | 12 AM | 17⌐
  Cyberport
Grill/Plateau | 24 hrs. | ‑⌐
  Wan Chai
Z Hutong | 12 AM | 24⌐
  Tsim Sha Tsui

Indonesian Rest. | 12 AM | **Causeway Bay** | 19

Jaspa's | 12 AM | **Soho** | 18

Little Sheep | 3 AM | **multi.** | 22

Mi-Ne | 12 AM | **Causeway Bay** | 18

Opia | 12 AM | **Causeway Bay** | 22

Petit Pomerol | 12 AM | **Causeway Bay** | -

Quarterdeck Club | 12 AM | **Tsim Sha Tsui** | 15

Stonegrill | 12:30 AM | **Soho** | 18

Tiffin Lounge | 12 AM | **Wan Chai** | 23

LOCAL FAVORITES

Bayside Brasserie | **Stanley** | 17

Bistro Manchu | **Soho** | 18

Bizou Bistro | **Soho** | 18

Boathouse | **Stanley** | 20

Café Landmark | **Central** | 16

China Tee | **Central** | 18

🛭 Crystal Jade | **Tsim Sha Tsui** | 23

Da Domenico | **Causeway Bay** | 26

Dim Sum | **Happy Valley** | 25

Di Vino | **Central** | 23

Farm House | **Causeway Bay** | 23

Jaspa's | **Soho** | 18

Jimmy's Kitchen | **Central** | 20

Life Café | **Soho** | 15

Luk Yu Tea | **Central** | 20

Maxim's | **Central** | 22

McSorley's | **Soho** | 11

Mi-Ne | **Causeway Bay** | 18

Modern China | **Causeway Bay** | -

Nha Trang | **Central** | 22

Peak Bar | **Soho** | 17

Peking Garden | **Tsim Sha Tsui** | 21

Tuk Tuk Thai | **Soho** | -

Wang Fu | **Central** | 21

🛭 Yung Kee | **Central** | 23

MEET FOR A DRINK

Agave | **Lan Kwai Fong** | 10

Al's Diner | **Lan Kwai Fong** | 17

Aqua | **Tsim Sha Tsui** | 19

Azure | **Lan Kwai Fong** | 19

Balalaika | **Lan Kwai Fong** | 16

Beirut | **Lan Kwai Fong** | 19

Boca Tapas | **Soho** | 20

Chinnery, The | **Central** | 23

Cinecittà | **Star Street** | 19

Dan Ryan's | **Admiralty** | 16

Di Vino | **Central** | 23

Dragon-I | **Central** | 18

🛭 Felix | **Tsim Sha Tsui** | 21

FINDS | **Lan Kwai Fong** | 17

Isola | **Central** | 22

Kee Club | **Lan Kwai Fong** | 20

Lumiere | **Central** | 18

McSorley's | **Soho** | 11

Opia | **Causeway Bay** | 22

Peak Bar | **Soho** | 17

Quarterdeck Club | **Wan Chai** | 15

NEW 798 Unit | **Causeway Bay** | 16

Wasabisabi | **Causeway Bay** | 19

Yun Fu | **Central** | 19

NEW Zuma | **Central** | 24

NOTEWORTHY NEWCOMERS

Agnès B. | **Causeway Bay** | 15

Bricolage 62 | **Soho** | 18

La Mer | **Lan Kwai Fong** | -

🛭 L'Atelier/Robuchon | **Central** | 27

Lian | **Central** | 20

🛭 Nobu | **Tsim Sha Tsui** | 25

Pearl on Peak | **The Peak** 19
Press Room | **Sheung Wan** 20
798 Unit | **Causeway Bay** 16
Wagyu | **Central** 22
Zest | **Central** 22
Zuma | **Central** 24

OUTDOOR DINING

(G=garden; P=patio; S=sidewalk;
T=terrace; W=waterside)

Boathouse | P, T | **Stanley** 20
Chilli N Spice | P, W | **Stanley** 19
Cinecittà | S | **Star Street** 19
Cococabana | T, W |
Deep Water Bay 16
Dirty Duck | T | **Wan Chai** -
Di Vino | T | **Central** 23
Dragon-I | P | **Central** 18
FINDS | P | **Lan Kwai Fong** 17
Fish Bar | P, W | **Admiralty** 20
Gaia | P | **Sheung Wan** 25
Gough 40 | S | **Sheung Wan** -
Grill/Plateau | W | **Wan Chai** -
Isola | P, W | **Central** 22
Jumbo | P, W |
Wong Chuk Hang 16
Kin's Kitchen | P | **North Point** 22
NEW La Mer | T |
Lan Kwai Fong -
Life Café | P | **Soho** 15
McSorley's | T | **Lantau Island** 11
One-Thirtyone | P, W | **Sai Kung** -
Peak Lookout | G, T | **The Peak** 17
NEW Pearl on Peak | T |
The Peak 19
Quarterdeck Club | T |
Wan Chai 15
RED | P | **Central** 15
Scirocco | T | **Soho** 23

Stoep, The | W | **Cheung Sha** 19
NEW Zuma | T | **Central** 24

PEOPLE-WATCHING

Agave | **Lan Kwai Fong** 10
Al's Diner | **Lan Kwai Fong** 17
Bizou Bistro | **Soho** 18
Café Landmark | **Central** 16
Cinecittà | **Star Street** 19
Dragon-I | **Central** 18
FINDS | **Lan Kwai Fong** 17
Frog Faced Fish | **Central** 16
Gaia | **Sheung Wan** 25
Gough 40 | **Sheung Wan** -
Peak Bar | **Soho** 17
Scirocco | **Soho** 23
NEW Wagyu | **Central** 22

POWER SCENES

Amber | **Central** 22
Azure | **Lan Kwai Fong** 19
Z Caprice | **Central** 25
Z China Club | **Central** 22
Ciprani's | **Central** 23
Cova | **Causeway Bay** 19
Z Gaddi's | **Tsim Sha Tsui** 27
Harlan's | **Central** 20
Ingredients | **Star Street** 16
Isola | **Central** 22
Jimmy's Kitchen | **Central** 20
Kee Club | **Lan Kwai Fong** 20
Kenjo's | **Tsim Sha Tsui** 29
Z NEW L'Atelier/Robuchon |
Central 27
Z Lung King Heen | **Central** 28
Mandarin Grill | **Central** 25
Man Wah | **Central** 26
Nadaman | **Admiralty** 26

Z **NEW** Nobu | **Tsim Sha Tsui** 25

Z Petrus | **Admiralty** 27

Ruth's Chris | **Tsim Sha Tsui** 21

PRIVATE ROOMS

(Restaurants charge less at off times; call for capacity)

Aqua | **Tsim Sha Tsui** 19

Z China Club | **Central** 22

Z Gaddi's | **Tsim Sha Tsui** 27

Magnolia | **Sheung Wan** 25

Z **NEW** Nobu | **Tsim Sha Tsui** 25

1 Harbour Road | **Wan Chai** 25

Opia | **Causeway Bay** 22

NEW Press Room | **Sheung Wan** 20

PRIX FIXE MENUS

(Call for prices and times)

NEW Agnès B. | **Causeway Bay** 15

Amaroni's | **Kowloon Tong** 15

Azure | **Lan Kwai Fong** 19

Babek | **Soho** –

Bo Innovation | **Central** 20

Z Caprice | **Central** 25

Frog Faced Fish | **Central** 16

Z Gaddi's | **Tsim Sha Tsui** 27

Inagiku | **Central** 25

Magnolia | **Sheung Wan** 25

Mandarin Grill | **Central** 25

One-Thirtyone | **Sai Kung** –

RED | **Central** 15

Tribute | **Soho** 22

Verandah | **Repulse Bay** 21

Yellow Door | **Soho** 19

QUICK BITES

Al's Diner | **Lan Kwai Fong** 17

Mi-Ne | **Causeway Bay** 18

Nha Trang | **Central** 22

Peak Bar | **Soho** 17

NEW 798 Unit | **Causeway Bay** 16

Shake 'Em Buns | **Star Street** 17

QUIET CONVERSATION

Amber | **Central** 22

Z Caprice | **Central** 25

Clipper Lounge | **Central** 22

Cova | **Causeway Bay** 19

Z Gaddi's | **Tsim Sha Tsui** 27

Lumiere | **Central** 18

M/Fringe | **Central** 24

Petit Pomerol | **Causeway Bay** –

Z Petrus | **Admiralty** 27

ROMANTIC PLACES

NEW Agnès B. | **Causeway Bay** 15

Amber | **Central** 22

Amigo | **Happy Valley** 22

Aqua | **Tsim Sha Tsui** 19

Azure | **Lan Kwai Fong** 19

Z Caprice | **Central** 25

Chez Patrick | **multi.** 20

Cococabana | **Deep Water Bay** 16

Cova | **Causeway Bay** 19

Dirty Duck | **Wan Chai** –

Z Felix | **Tsim Sha Tsui** 21

Z Gaddi's | **Tsim Sha Tsui** 27

Gaia | **Sheung Wan** 25

Gough 40 | **Sheung Wan** –

Grill/Plateau | **Wan Chai** –

Grissini | **Wan Chai** 23

Habitu | **Causeway Bay** 14

Isola | **Central** 22

Lumiere | **Central** 18

M/Fringe | **Central** 24
Nicholini's | **Admiralty** 23
One-Thirtyone | **Sai Kung** -
Peak Lookout | **The Peak** 17
NEW Pearl on Peak | **The Peak** 19
Petit Pomerol | **Causeway Bay** -
Z Petrus | **Admiralty** 27
Tribute | **Soho** 22
Verandah | **Repulse Bay** 21
NEW Zuma | **Central** 24

SINGLES SCENES

Agave | **Lan Kwai Fong** 10
Al's Diner | **Lan Kwai Fong** 17
Azure | **Lan Kwai Fong** 19
Boca Tapas | **Soho** 20
Cinecittà | **Star Street** 19
Di Vino | **Central** 23
Z Felix | **Tsim Sha Tsui** 21
FINDS | **Lan Kwai Fong** 17
Habitu | **Causeway Bay** 14
Isola | **Central** 22
Kee Club | **Lan Kwai Fong** 20
Opia | **Causeway Bay** 22
Peak Bar | **Soho** 17
Quarterdeck Club | **Wan Chai** 15
NEW Zuma | **Central** 24

SPECIAL OCCASIONS

Amigo | **Happy Valley** 22
Aqua | **Tsim Sha Tsui** 19
Z Caprice | **Central** 25
Ciprani's | **Central** 23
Cococabana | **Deep Water Bay** 16
Da Ping Huo | **Soho** 24
Z Felix | **Tsim Sha Tsui** 21
Grill/Plateau | **Wan Chai** -

Z NEW L'Atelier/Robuchon | **Central** 27
Magnolia | **Sheung Wan** 25
M/Fringe | **Central** 24
Z NEW Nobu | **Tsim Sha Tsui** 25
One-Thirtyone | **Sai Kung** -
Peak Lookout | **The Peak** 17
NEW Pearl on Peak | **The Peak** 19
Peking Garden | **Tsim Sha Tsui** 21
Z Spoon | **Tsim Sha Tsui** 23
Verandah | **Repulse Bay** 21
Z Yung Kee | **Central** 23
NEW Zuma | **Central** 24

TRANSPORTING EXPERIENCES

Bo Innovation | **Central** 20
Cococabana | **Deep Water Bay** 16
Da Ping Huo | **Soho** 24
Z Felix | **Tsim Sha Tsui** 21
Green T. House | **Cyberport** 17
Jumbo | **Wong Chuk Hang** 16
Magnolia | **Sheung Wan** 25
Maxim's | **Central** 22
One-Thirtyone | **Sai Kung** -
Stoep, The | **Cheung Sha** 19

TRENDY

NEW Agnès B. | **Causeway Bay** 15
Aqua | **Tsim Sha Tsui** 19
Azure | **Lan Kwai Fong** 19
Dragon-I | **Central** 18
Z Felix | **Tsim Sha Tsui** 21
FINDS | **Lan Kwai Fong** 17
Gaia | **Sheung Wan** 25
Green T. House | **Cyberport** 17
Habitu | **Causeway Bay** 14
Ingredients | **Star Street** 16

Isola | **Central** 22
Kee Club | **Lan Kwai Fong** 20
Z NEW L'Atelier/Robuchon | **Central** 27
NEW Lian | **Central** 20
Lumiere | **Central** 18
Mi-Ne | **Causeway Bay** 18
Modern China | **Causeway Bay** -
Z NEW Nobu | **Tsim Sha Tsui** 25
Opia | **Causeway Bay** 22
Song Cuisine | **Soho** 22
Z Spoon | **Tsim Sha Tsui** 23
NEW Wagyu | **Central** 22
NEW Zuma | **Central** 24

VIEWS

Aqua | **Tsim Sha Tsui** 19
Azure | **Lan Kwai Fong** 19
Bayside Brasserie | **Stanley** 17
Boathouse | **Stanley** 20
Cafe Deco | **The Peak** 18
Z Caprice | **Central** 25
Z China Club | **Central** 22
Cococabana | **Deep Water Bay** 16
Cuisine Cuisine | **Central** 18
Z Felix | **Tsim Sha Tsui** 21
Grill/Plateau | **Wan Chai** -
Grissini | **Wan Chai** 23
Z Hutong | **Tsim Sha Tsui** 24
Inagiku | **Central** 25
Isola | **Central** 22
Jumbo | **Wong Chuk Hang** 16
Lumiere | **Central** 18
Z Lung King Heen | **Central** 28
Mandarin Grill | **Central** 25
Man Wah | **Central** 26
Morton's | **Tsim Sha Tsui** 26
Nadaman | **Admiralty** 26

New Dynasty | **Wan Chai** -
Nicholini's | **Admiralty** 23
Z NEW Nobu | **Tsim Sha Tsui** 25
1 Harbour Road | **Wan Chai** 25
One-Thirtyone | **Sai Kung** -
Peak Lookout | **The Peak** 17
NEW Pearl on Peak | **The Peak** 19
Peking Garden | **Tsim Sha Tsui** 21
Z Petrus | **Admiralty** 27
RED | **Central** 15
Rice Paper | **Tsim Sha Tsui** 18
Z Spoon | **Tsim Sha Tsui** 23
Steak House | **Tsim Sha Tsui** 25
Stoep, The | **Cheung Sha** 19
Tott's | **Causeway Bay** -
Verandah | **Repulse Bay** 21
Z Yan Toh Heen | **Tsim Sha Tsui** 26

VISITORS ON EXPENSE ACCOUNT

Amber | **Central** 22
Bo Innovation | **Central** 20
Da Domenico | **Causeway Bay** 26
Z Felix | **Tsim Sha Tsui** 21
Z Gaddi's | **Tsim Sha Tsui** 27
Harlan's | **Central** 20
Inagiku | **Central** 25
Ingredients | **Star Street** 16
Kee Club | **Lan Kwai Fong** 20
Kenjo's | **Tsim Sha Tsui** 29
Z NEW L'Atelier/Robuchon | **Central** 27
Morton's | **Tsim Sha Tsui** 26
Z NEW Nobu | **Tsim Sha Tsui** 25
NEW Pearl on Peak | **The Peak** 19
Petit Pomerol | **Causeway Bay** -
Ruth's Chris | **Tsim Sha Tsui** 21
Z Spoon | **Tsim Sha Tsui** 23

DINING

SPECIAL FEATURES

WINNING WINE LISTS

Amber | **Central**	22
Z Caprice | **Central**	25
Ciprani's | **Central**	23
Di Vino | **Central**	23
Z Felix | **Tsim Sha Tsui**	21
Z Gaddi's | **Tsim Sha Tsui**	27
Gaia | **Sheung Wan**	25
Grissini | **Wan Chai**	23
Harlan's | **Central**	20
Ingredients | **Star Street**	16
Isola | **Central**	22
Kee Club | **Lan Kwai Fong**	20
Z NEW L'Atelier/Robuchon | **Central**	27
Z Lung King Heen | **Central**	28
Mandarin Grill | **Central**	25
Z NEW Nobu | **Tsim Sha Tsui**	25
Petit Pomerol | **Causeway Bay**	–
Z Petrus | **Admiralty**	27
NEW Press Room | **Sheung Wan**	20
Ruth's Chris | **Tsim Sha Tsui**	21
Z Spoon | **Tsim Sha Tsui**	23
NEW Zuma | **Central**	24

Hotel Locations

Includes hotel names and Room ratings.

ADMIRALTY

Conrad   25
☑ Island Shangri-La   26
JW Marriott   22

CAUSEWAY BAY

Excelsior, The   16
Jia   -
Park Lane   -

CENTRAL

☑ Four Seasons   29
NEW Hotel LKF   -
Lan Kwai Fong Hotel   -
☑ Mandarin Oriental   25
Mandarin Oriental Landmark   26

CHEK LAP KOK

Regal Airport   16

CYBERPORT

Le Méridien   26

HUNG HOM

Harbour Plaza   -

LANTAU ISLAND

Disneyland Hotel   23

MONGKOK

Langham Place   24

SHATIN

Royal Park   -

TSIM SHA TSUI

Eaton   17
Holiday Inn   15
InterContinental   25
InterContinental Grand Stanford   23
Kowloon Shangri-La   23
Langham   20
NEW Luxe Manor   -
Marco Polo   15
Miramar   -
Nikko   18
☑ Peninsula   28
Renaissance Kowloon   -
Royal Garden   -
Salisbury YMCA   -
Sheraton   21

TUNG CHUNG

Novotel-Citygate   -

WAN CHAI

Cosmo   -
Grand Hyatt   24
Renaissance Harbor View   19

Hotel Special Features

Listings cover the best in each category and include hotel names, locations and Room ratings. ⚡ indicates places with the highest ratings, popularity and importance.

BOUTIQUE

Cosmo | **Wan Chai** – |
NEW Hotel LKF | **Central** – |
Jia | **Causeway Bay** – |
Lan Kwai Fong Hotel | **Central** – |
NEW Luxe Manor | **Tsim Sha Tsui** – |
Mandarin Oriental Landmark | **Central** 26 |

BUSINESS-ORIENTED

Conrad | **Admiralty** 25 |
Excelsior, The | **Causeway Bay** 16 |
Grand Hyatt | **Wan Chai** 24 |
⚡ Island Shangri-La | **Admiralty** 26 |
JW Marriott | **Admiralty** 22 |
⚡ Mandarin Oriental | **Central** 25 |
Nikko | **Tsim Sha Tsui** 18 |
Park Lane | **Causeway Bay** – |
Regal Airport | **Chek Lap Kok** 16 |
Renaissance Harbor View | **Wan Chai** 19 |

CITY VIEWS

Conrad | **Admiralty** 25 |
Cosmo | **Wan Chai** – |
Excelsior, The | **Causeway Bay** 16 |
⚡ Four Seasons | **Central** 29 |
Harbour Plaza | **Hung Hom** – |
Holiday Inn | **Tsim Sha Tsui** 15 |
InterContinental | **Tsim Sha Tsui** 25 |
InterContinental Grand Stanford | **Tsim Sha Tsui** 23 |

BOUTIQUE (continued)

⚡ Island Shangri-La | **Admiralty** 26 |
Jia | **Causeway Bay** – |
JW Marriott | **Admiralty** 22 |
Kowloon Shangri-La | **Tsim Sha Tsui** 23 |
Langham | **Tsim Sha Tsui** 20 |
Langham Place | **Mongkok** 24 |
⚡ Mandarin Oriental | **Central** 25 |
Marco Polo | **Tsim Sha Tsui** 15 |
⚡ Peninsula | **Tsim Sha Tsui** 28 |
Sheraton | **Tsim Sha Tsui** 21 |

DINING EXCELLENCE

⚡ Four Seasons | **Central** 29 |
InterContinental | **Tsim Sha Tsui** 25 |
⚡ Island Shangri-La | **Admiralty** 26 |
⚡ Mandarin Oriental | **Central** 25 |
Mandarin Oriental Landmark | **Central** 26 |
⚡ Peninsula | **Tsim Sha Tsui** 28 |
Sheraton | **Tsim Sha Tsui** 21 |

DRAMATIC DESIGN

Cosmo | **Wan Chai** – |
InterContinental | **Tsim Sha Tsui** 25 |
Jia | **Causeway Bay** – |
Langham Place | **Mongkok** 24 |
Lan Kwai Fong Hotel | **Central** – |
NEW Luxe Manor | **Tsim Sha Tsui** – |
⚡ Mandarin Oriental | **Central** 25 |
Mandarin Oriental Landmark | **Central** 26 |
⚡ Peninsula | **Tsim Sha Tsui** 28 |